A GRAPHICALLY EXPLICIT PAPERBACK

★ ★ ★ ★ ★

LEARN NEW SKILLS

TECHNICAL & BUSINESS WRITING

FOR EVERYONE WHO WANTS TO IMPROVE THEIR WRITING AT WORK

ANDREW ALLEN MOORE

AN EXPLICIT GUIDE TO WRITING PROFESSIONAL DOCUMENTS

Copyright

Copyright © 2024 Andrew Allen Moore. All rights reserved.

This publication may not, in whole or in part, be reproduced, transmitted, transcribed, stored in a retrieval system, or translated in any form or by any means without prior written consent of Andrew Allen Moore.

Liability

The authors have used their best efforts to ensure that the content of this document is useful and correct at the time of publication. The content of this document is supplied for information only and is subject to change without notice. The authors assume no responsibility or liability for any errors or inaccuracies that may appear in this document, nor the use to which it may be put.

Publishing Information

Author:	Andrew Allen Moore
Published by:	AAM Design
Website:	www.aamdesign.co.uk
Publication Number:	AAM-003
First Published:	November 2024
Issue Number:	1
Issue Date:	November 2024

Contents

INTRODUCTION 5
   1. About this Book 6
   2. Creating 'Good' & 'Bad' Documentation 8
   3. 'Good' or 'Bad'; Why Does it Matter? 10

DOCUMENT PLANNING 12
   4. Delivering the Right Document 13
   5. Writing to Influence or Persuade 15
   6. Writing to Inform or Educate 17
   7. Writing to Instruct or Capture a Process 19
   8. Writing a Report 21
   9. Writing a Reference Document 23
   10. Writing Web Content 25
   11. Identifying Your Readers 27
   12. Writing for an Internal Audience 29
   13. Writing for an External Audience 31
   14. Assessing the Scope of Your Document 33
   15. Structuring Your Document 35
   16. Formatting Your Document 37
   17. Designing a Stylesheet 39
   18. Using Information Design Techniques 41
   19. Using Graphic Design Techniques 43
   20. Calculating Time-to-Completion 45
   21. Delivering On Time 47
   22. Delivering To-Budget 49
   23. Delivering Your Plan 51

DOCUMENT DESIGN 53
   24. Choosing the Right Tool for the Right Job 54
   25. Designing for Print 56
   26. Designing for PDF 58
   27. Designing for Help 60
   28. Designing for Presentation 62
   29. Designing for Translation 64

INFORMATION GATHERING 66
- 30. Collecting Source Information 67
- 31. Asking for Input 69

DOCUMENT WRITING 71
- 32. Is Your English Good-Enough? 72
- 33. Thinking of the Writer 74
- 34. Thinking of the Reader 76
- 35. Starting Writing 78
- 36. Crafting Your First Draft 80
- 37. Choosing the Right Language 82
- 38. Writing Captivating Headings 84
- 39. Choosing the Right Words 86
- 40. Choosing Concise Words & Phrases 88
- 41. Writing Engaging Sentences 90
- 42. Writing Purposeful Paragraphs 92
- 43. Writing Effective Instructions 94
- 44. Writing Training Materials 96
- 45. Writing for the UK & US 98

DOCUMENT IMAGES 100
- 46. Including Meaningful Images 101
- 47. Understanding Images 103
- 48. Retouching Your Images 105

REVIEWING & EDITING 107
- 49. Editing Your First Draft 108
- 50. Completing Your First Draft 110
- 51. Chasing Perfection 112

DOCUMENT MANAGEMENT 114
- 52. Keeping Track of Your Document 115
- 53. The Document Lifecycle 117
- 54. Troubleshooting a Bad Document 119
- 55. Why Bother with Good Documentation? 121
- What Have You Done? 123
- About the Author 124

INTRODUCTION

1. About this Book

Why You Need to Read this Book

If you're reading this, I assume you're feeling less than confident about writing. I also assume you're not a trained writer and your background is in some other field of expertise, such as software, marketing, accountancy, science, administration or engineering. Me too.

Perhaps you've been asked to create a presentation, a booklet, a report, a proposal, a datasheet or even a product user manual; and you're not sure how to go about it. In this book, I also assume your knowledge of grammar is basic and your experience of formal writing is minimal or non-existent.

Don't panic. Writing professionally doesn't mean you have to have a degree in English literature, journalism or creative writing and you don't need to be an expert in grammar.

All you need are two things:

- **ATTITUDE** ("*I am going to make an effort*"), and
- **APPRECIATION** ("*I recognise good writing when I read it*").

Read on and, hopefully, all will become clear.

What this Book IS and IS NOT

This book is not an in-depth treatise of technical or business writing and does not contain templates for business proposals or standard forms of letter. Other publications are available for that. So what is this book about?

In this book you'll discover:

- Why everyone needs to be able to write professionally.
- How to acquire the skills of a professional writer.
- What to consider when writing a professional document.
- Why it is important to plan any documentation project.

- How to plan a documentation project.
- What to include in a documentation plan.
- How to structure a document to help your readers find information quickly.
- How to format a document so it looks professional, makes the content comprehensible and makes it memorable.
- How to write content to keep your readers engaged.
- How to write for diverse audiences and different purposes.
- How to publish and maintain documents through a '*lifecycle*' of creation, revision and retirement.

Documents You Might Be Asked to Write at Work

Here's a list (by no means exhaustive) of documents you might be asked to write as an employee, a manager or a director of a business, and for which this book will be useful:

- Memoranda.
- Business emails.
- Bids and business proposals.
- Powerpoint presentations.
- Technical or scientific reports.
- Operator/user guides.
- Servicing/maintenance manuals.
- Installation/assembly instructions.
- Product or component specifications/datasheets.
- Training documentation.
- Testing regimes, specifications and instructions.
- Software release notes.
- Work instructions for business processes.

2. Creating 'Good' & 'Bad' Documentation

What is 'Bad' Documentation?

In 30-plus years of working for engineering and technology companies, I've seen countless bad documents. By *'bad'* I mean documents that are poorly written, ineffective, confusing, unclear, inaccurate, outdated or that contain numerous mistakes and inconsistencies. In fact, bad documentation seems to be the accepted norm.

Why is 'Bad' Documentation the Accepted Norm?

If your company has no documentation standards and no one with overall responsibility for checking the standard of documents it delivers to its customers, this inevitably result in errors, inconsistencies, confusion and poor communication.

Documentation as an Afterthought

One reason for bad documentation is that it tends to be an afterthought. If the requirement for documentation is considered after a product or service has been developed, rather than at the start, or if it is left until an important business meeting is looming; then it will be produced in haste. That's never good.

Documentation by Untrained Staff

Another reason poor documentation is produced is that the person asked to write it has probably no training or little experience in writing professional documentation.

It's likely your company used to employ someone (a technical author, a bid writer, a graphic designer, a middle manager) who wrote documentation. These days, however, most companies have *'cut-back'* and *'down-sized'* to such an extent that they no longer employ dedicated document writers.

Now it's up to you (everyone, in fact) to write documents, in addition to your other duties. You have a computer on your desk. How hard can it be?

Documentation without Ownership & Accountibility

Documentation is often treated as a box-ticking exercise. The person requesting the document is concerned only with producing something (anything) by a deadline with no real understanding, interest or appreciation of what would really benefit the company.

The person being asked to write the document is often given vague instructions, a too-urgent deadline and is not encouraged to stop and think about what is really needed. The task becomes one of, *'How little can we get away with?'*

Documentation as a Low Priority

When a documentation task is imposed on someone who has other work to do (i.e. their day-job), it automatically becomes a low priority for them and something to be completed as quickly as possible. This is never going to result in good-enough documentation.

3. 'Good' or 'Bad'; Why Does it Matter?

The Consequences of 'Bad' Documentation

To see how important this is, and in case you or your boss needs persuading, let's consider the potential problems bad documentation may cause:

- If your document contains mistakes or isn't up-to-date, this could result in incorrect usage, or damage to, your product or service.
- If it's poorly written, this could affect customer confidence in your document, your product or service and your company.
- If it contains inconsistencies, this could make your product or service difficult to understand and use. This may result in calls and complaints to your customer support helpline.
- If it doesn't contain sufficient information that your customers need, important (and expensive) features may go undiscovered or under-utilised.
- If its structure is confusing, your customers may not be able to find what they are looking for, which may result in your document being discarded.
- If installation instructions are incomplete or contain errors, this may result in your customers not being able to install your product or service.
- If your document doesn't contain adequate troubleshooting information, your product or service may be off-line for longer than necessary, causing your customers grief.
- If it lacks appropriate health and safety information, your company may be held liable for accidents or injuries caused.

In short, '*bad*' documentation reflects badly on you (the author), your company and your company's products and services. Having considered the potential pitfalls, I hope you (and your boss) will agree that it's worth making an effort to do it well.

So What is 'Good' Documentation?

The benefits of good documentation should be unquestionably obvious to your reader, if you want to avoid it being ignored, abandoned or despised. So what are these benefits?

It should be interesting to read, but no longer than is necessary. It must provide information your readers are expecting as well as content they didn't know they needed. It should educate, support and explain complex ideas. It should provide solutions and suggestions when problems arise. Above all, it should be accurate, up-to-date, make your readers' job easier and save them time; thereby, compelling them to use it.

Checklist for 'Good' Documentation

Learning to write professional documentation requires thought and effort. Treat it as you would any other component part that has to be researched, designed, developed and manufactured:

1. Research the type of document needed.
2. Determine the expectation and requirement.
3. Decide what your document needs to cover.
4. Locate or define any documentation standards.
5. Create a prototype and a preliminary contents list.
6. Plan how much work is involved and how long it will take.
7. Distribute and get approval for your plan.
8. Research and gather source information.
9. Find the right experts (to contribute).
10. Use your best efforts to write good content.
11. Proofread your own draft.
12. Get experts to review your draft.
13. Generate more drafts, as necessary, to attain excellence.
14. Obtain approval and sign-off.
15. Identify and issue your document.
16. Publish and deliver the document according to your plan.

DOCUMENT PLANNING

4. Delivering the Right Document

Before you start writing, or even start planning to write, be clear about the '*design brief*' you've been given. If this was a verbal request, be sure to ask questions that clearly define the scale and scope of the task. This is essential to delivering the document everybody wants. Also, find out who is going to sign-off this document as complete and accurate. This is the person taking responsibility and who you are ultimately working for.

WHY is the Document Needed?

Only when you understand the purpose of the document can you produce the appropriate content and use the right language.

A new product may require a user manual, a data sheet or an installation guide to inform or educate its customers. Updated software features often need explaining to its users. A new manufacturing process may require operation and maintenance instructions for its assembly line workers. A business proposal may require a presentation to persuade a board of directors or the implementation team that an idea is worthwhile.

Whatever the purpose, information is passed from those who have it to those who don't. This transfer of knowledge is vital for the success of the product, service, system or idea.

WHO is the Document For?

Without an understanding of who the document is for, you won't know what topics to include in your document or how much detail to go into.

Research your target audience, their technical and business background and find out where and how they will use the document. Perhaps you will need to provide a summary or overview to help a less technical reader. Alternatively, technical detail could be separated out into a different section, chapter or document.

WHAT should the Document Contain?

Be certain what product model, software version or business process, your document must cover. State this explicitly at the start so your readers can be confident they're reading the right document.

Discuss the scope of your document with others who may have an opinion on this (including your boss), and find out what your customers want? If you can't speak to them directly, you'll have to put yourself in their position and consider what it is they need.

When you understand WHY the document is needed, WHO it is for and WHAT it should contain, you can start gathering information and planning your documentation.

HOW should your Document Look?

Getting the format and presentation right can greatly influence the effectiveness of your document. Investigate whether a company standard, house-style or template is available. Find out where you can get hold of company branding, templates, images and fonts.

If there isn't a suitable template available, this presents an opportunity for you to create one. Treat this as a separate documentation task before you start writing your document. The stylesheet/template will probably require approval from your marketing department, manager or director.

WHEN is the Document Required?

Delivering the right document at the right time is essential. It will probably have to coincide with a product launch, an important meeting or a system delivery.

When you've worked out how long your document will take to prepare and produce, work backwards from the product delivery deadline to calculate when you need to start. If you can't make that deadline you should flag this up now and prepare an alternative plan to shorten the production time (perhaps by having more than one author).

5. Writing to Influence or Persuade

If you're writing for decision makers or purchasers, your purpose is to convince them why your proposal is exactly what they need.

Be Authentic

In order to persuade, you must do it authentically with sincere conviction, which means knowing and believing that your product or service will genuinely benefit your readers (customers).

Write Compelling Content

Make your document an indispensable resource by considering what your readers need, and by writing essential content that engages with them personally. Simplify complex detail and support your readers with concise and clear information.

Present a Clear Choice

Include sufficient information for your readers to make a business decision or purchase. Don't waste their time, and yours, by padding-out your content. Incorporate the essential detail your readers require, and no more.

Anticipate Your Readers' Questions

Answering your readers' questions before they ask them demonstrates that you understand their requirements, problems and priorities. This will establish your credibility.

Establish Trust

Give your readers confidence that they're making the right decision by including examples or a case study to demonstrate how your solutions have successfully helped others with similar requirements. Perhaps your company can offer a guarantee or a trial offer as proof of confidence in the product or service.

Appeal to Emotions

Persuasion is best accomplished by appealing to emotions. Using emotive language and content speaks to your readers personally and engages their emotions as well as their intellect.

Appeal to Aspirations

Make your presentation appealing and appropriate for your intended audience by utilising graphic design techniques and suitable colour, fonts, white space and images.

Stress the Benefits, NOT the Features

You cannot simply list the features of your product or service in the hope that your readers will realise how good it is. Don't assume its benefits are obvious. What do your readers care about? Will it save them time? Will it make them more effective? Will it solve their problems?

Use Bullets & Illustrations Appropriately

List the benefits, the features, the reasons, but don't overuse bullets in a situation where a diagram would give a better understanding, clarify a relationship or explain a process. A bulleted list should stand out on the page and draw attention to important items.

Call to Action

Finish your presentation with a call to action: '*Call us today*', '*Buy this product in three easy steps*', '*Contact us for details of offers*', etc. If your readers don't respond immediately, have a back-up response prepared: a free download or newsletter to establish contact. Always give them something to remember you by.

6. Writing to Inform or Educate

If you're writing to communicate knowledge, then your purpose is to present information in a way that's easy for your audience to understand, absorb and remember.

Identify Your Subject & Your Purpose

Attract interested readers by clearly identifying the subject of your document, i.e. be clear which type, model or version of your product, service or proposal it relates to. Also be clear about what aspect it covers, i.e. installation, operation, servicing, etc., so your readers can assess whether it contains information they want.

Give Your Subject Context

Introduce the subject with an overview of the big picture or system into which the subject fits to set the context. Details are always easier to understand and remember if we know how they fit into the overall scheme of things.

Write Flowing Content

Write content that presents information functionally, sequentially or logically, as appropriate. Content should flow naturally from input to output, from start to finish or from large to small.

Organise Your Content

Don't dump everything you know about a subject in the same place; it's unlikely your readers will want to know, or be able to absorb, everything all at once.

Use chapters, sections and headings to arrange your content into categories or types (installation, setting up, configuration, operation, monitoring, maintenance, etc.). Provide an intuitive structure by breaking up content into manageable chunks that are easy to understand and absorb.

Summarise/Review

A summary at the end of a section or chapter can be useful in a technical or complex document to ensure your readers have grasped the main points before moving on to the next section.

Provide Clear Navigation

In a lengthy document (of 30 pages or more), finding and revisiting topics becomes difficult. Consider using running page headers/footers, table and figure numbering, and provide a table of contents and/or an index to aid navigation, save time and ensure your readers don't have to re-read the entire document.

Use Appropriate Language

When you've written a significant paragraph or section, read it back and analyse each sentence to see if it can be rewritten in fewer, or simpler, words without loss of information.

Get the Pace Right

Deliver the detail your readers need, when they need it. Present facts at a pace they will be able to absorb, rather than blurting out everything all at once. Ensure your facts are well-researched and provide references for your sources, where appropriate.

Get the Level Right

Be sure you are writing at the right level of detail for your readers. Know your audience, their background, education and training and leave out irrelevant technicalities or complexities.

Use Questions to Encourage Thinking

Using questions as headings is an effective technique for stimulating your readers' thought processes and engaging them in active, rather than passive, reading. Your mind always responds to a question, doesn't it?

7. Writing to Instruct or Capture a Process

If you're writing a procedure to describe how to use a product or service, then your purpose is to present instructions clearly, concisely and safely and, of course, in the correct sequence.

Evaluate the Importance of Procedures

Procedures are necessary for most processes whether important, lengthy, complex or routine. It's essential that everyone performs the procedure consistently, efficiently, effectively and safely to avoid the consequences of doing it wrong.

Define the Scope

Be specific when describing what your procedure relates to. This ensures your readers don't discover part-way through that they are using the wrong one.

Write Sequential Instructions

Procedures should be written in a sequential, step-by-step manner. Don't make statements after the fact, such as: "*Make sure you turn off the power first*". This could be dangerous and costly.

Use Numbers NOT Bullets

When writing step-by-step instructions, always format as numerically numbered '*ordered*' paragraphs, rather than as bulleted '*unordered*' ones. Be clear this is not a menu list from which you can pick and choose.

Be Precise

Choose your words carefully so there's no ambiguity or uncertainty. This will reduce the possibility of mistakes. Always look for better words rather than adding more words to clarify what you really mean.

Include Meaningful Images

Use photographs, screenshots, illustrations or diagrams with appropriate annotations, to identify parts or sequential processes, which would otherwise be difficult or lengthy to convey in words.

Include Warnings, Cautions & Notes

If you're instructing someone to perform a sequence of actions, you're also responsible for their health and safety. Always include appropriate warnings and/or cautions prior to each step:

- **Warnings** – Present a danger to life or health
- **Cautions** – Could cause damage, an outage or reduced performance of the equipment or system
- **Notes** – Note-worthy asides that your readers might want to be aware of, but they do not affect their health and safety.

Avoid Repetition

Rather than repeating a series of steps (a partial sequence), it may be useful to pull out these steps as a separate sub-procedure you can refer to. This avoids errors in consistency and makes alterations straightforward by updating the sub-procedure rather than having to locate and update multiple occurrences within other procedures.

Test Your Instructions

Verify your procedure is accurate by testing it out or by getting someone else to do it for you. You will (nearly always) discover errors to be corrected and missing detail to be included.

Separate Your (How to...) Instructions

Always separate descriptions (the '*WHAT*') from the processes (the '*HOW*') in separate sections or chapters. Anyone looking to find how to use your product, service or system does not want to wade through lengthy descriptions of what it is, and what it will do.

8. Writing a Report

As with a lot of technical or business writing, your purpose when writing a report is to present an impartial, objective and factual account.

Know Your Brief

Be sure to discuss the content of the report with the person giving you the brief, and with any other interested parties, to ensure you deliver the report everyone is expecting.

Discuss the Good, the Bad & the Indifferent

A report should be an unbiased investigation of a topic. You must endeavour to provide an objective analysis from all the data collected. If some data was inconclusive, you need to mention that too. Be careful NOT to include your own opinions, feelings or bias. You should reach an unprejudiced conclusion based on the information presented with recommendations for possible action.

Be Clear & Precise

When writing a report, be clear in your writing, precise in your detailing of facts, and comprehensive in the presentation of your information. Your report should be easy to read and understandable to someone with little knowledge of the subject.

Find out Whether to use 'Passive' or 'Active' Voice

Traditionally, the more formal *'third-person'* (*'it'*, *'it's'*, *'itself'*) and the passive voice (*"It is recommended that..."*) are used in reports to suggest objectivity.

Some organisations, however, allow a *'first-person'* approach (*'I'*, *'my'*, *'myself'*) and the active voice (*"I recommend..."*) for a personal and punchier prose style. Find out which style your company prefers.

Define the Report Structure

Report structures vary among disciplines and companies. Check whether a company template already exists, or whether reports have been produced previously.

A typical report structure typically includes the following sections:

- **Title Page.** Report title, author(s) names and roles, publication details.
- **Abstract.** A short summary of the report's content (for those who don't want to read the whole thing).
- **Table of Contents.** A list of the main headings (so your readers can go straight to the content they're interested in).
- **Introduction.** Terms of reference, scope, a brief outline of the method and background to the report.
- **Methodology.** How you carried out the enquiry and the method you used in collecting data.
- **Results.** A detailed section with data translated into diagrams, graphs and tables, for ease of understanding.
- **Discussion.** A discussion of the key findings, explanations, and any problems encountered.
- **Conclusions & Recommendations.** An unbiased conclusion with recommended actions to be taken.
- **Appendices.** References and supporting information. Not essential but included for completeness (if anyone wants to check your facts and sources).

9. Writing a Reference Document

If you're writing a factual reference document, i.e. something that's not read from cover-to-cover, such as a parts list, a software commands document or a product catalogue, your purpose is to make that information clear, succinct and easy to find.

Organise Your Document Appropriately

Determine the best way to organise, structure and present the information. Should it be logical, functional, hierarchical, sequential, chronological, alphabetical, or use a different scheme?

Format Your Document Appropriately

Design an appropriate format for the content you're presenting. Does it require lists or descriptive paragraphs? Would a textual or a graphical approach be best? Always ask yourself, "*Is there a better way to present this information?*"

Find Out How the Document will be Used

Knowing *how* and *where* the document will be used may help you to get the format and presentation right. It might suggest a small or large printed document, or an online one. If read outdoors, will there be Wi-Fi access or will it need to be downloaded? If the detail is small, such as wiring diagrams, will it be visible and usable on a mobile phone or tablet?

Provide Clear Navigation

Use elements such as running headers, headings, numbering, contents lists, and an index or glossary to help your readers find information quickly. Signpost sections clearly and consider using graphics, symbols or colour to highlight sections and make them identifiable when flicking through the document.

Add Value to Your Document

Writing a good reference document means adding value for your readers. Analyse, simplify and translate complex source information into clearer and more comprehensible content.

Use Tables, Charts, Graphs & Illustrations

Sometimes a picture, a table or chart can bring clarity to a mass of numbers, statistics or a lengthy description. Consider this if it would make the information easier to comprehend or memorise.

Check Your Facts

In a reference document, the information it contains must be accurate; your readers are relying on this to do their jobs. Make an extra effort to check and review your content.

Utilise Guides, Tutorials & Examples

Reference documents can be complex, technical and lengthy. By incorporating guides, tutorials and examples you can make it accessible to a wider audience.

Optimise Your Pagination

In a lengthy document, font sizes and paragraph spacing choices can make a significant difference to the length of your document. A little squeezing may reduce the page count and should be considered, but don't make it difficult to read by using text that is too small or paragraphs that are visibly compressed.

Get an Expert to Check Your Work

You don't need to be an expert to write a reference document. Be sure, however, to have your document reviewed by a qualified, knowledgeable and experienced expert.

10. Writing Web Content

Readers *scan* rather than *read* web content because reading words on a screen is slower, harder and more fatiguing. Your purpose, therefore, is to grab their attention and quickly direct them to the information they want. If your website doesn't do this, your readers will lose patience and move on.

Identify Your Readers' Objectives

People come to your website with a specific objective. Put yourself in their position and imagine what that might be. Create the content that will help them achieve their objective. Don't generate content to suit you or your company; think of your readers.

Hook Your Readers with Questions

People will come to your website with specific questions in mind. Using questions as headings will engage your readers by creating an interaction between you and them. It's also a good method for guiding your readers' thought processes, getting them to think through the possibilities and encouraging them to delve deeper.

Use (Key) Words Your Readers' will Search For

Use an online keyword tool to see what words in your content rank as popular. You can then incorporate them into your headings and repeat in your content but don't overdo it, as overuse can be detrimental to your search ranking.

Write for Humans, NOT Search Engines

There are no clever loopholes or magic formulae to outwit a search engine, so don't bother trying. Always write for humans first and search engines second.

Write Like a Journalist

Place essential, important, interesting or surprising content at the beginning (top) of your article. Having captured your readers' attention, deliver the detail or explanation they are now craving in subsequent paragraphs or in links to other web pages.

Keep it Short

Use concise headings, short sentences, succinct paragraphs and small lists, so information can be quickly absorbed. Get to the point and avoid lengthy and rambling *'marketing-speak'*.

Use a Casual Conversational Tone

Keep your content friendly and relatable by addressing your readers as *'you'* and by using abbreviations that are spoken in casual conversation, such as: *'you're'* (you are), *'you'll'* (you will), *'you'd'* (you would), and *'can't'* (cannot), etc.

Keep Your Language Simple

In general, aim to write for an inexpert audience by not using jargon (or explaining it simply if you do) and by using commonly used words and straightforward language. Note that this is not the same as dumbing-down.

Provide a 'You Are Here' Flag

Don't assume your readers know what your website, blog or content is about or how to find their way around. If they follow your links or scroll down a long page, give them clear navigation to let them know where they are and how to get back.

Don't Forget to Check Your Work

Web content is visible to the whole world, so it pays to check your work before publishing online. To avoid embarrassment, always check your facts and your writing before uploading.

11. Identifying Your Readers

Who Do You Think You're Talking To?

To engage your readers, you must appeal to them directly by providing content they're interested in and by writing to a level of detail they can understand and absorb.

It's essential to know who your readers are and what their knowledge, skills, experience and expectations are. Once you understand this, you'll be able to write compelling documents for your intended audience.

Writing to a Level

It's tempting to jump right in and write at the level of complexity the subject demands. However, if you're writing for readers who are not technically savvy and your content is too complex from the start, they may have difficulty understanding and be overwhelmed. Guide your readers by starting with something they know and introducing complexity at a pace they can absorb.

If writing for technical or scientific readers, you probably can, and should, write at their technical level from the start. If your writing is too basic or insubstantial, there's a chance they'll quickly get bored and abandon it altogether.

Writing for the Individual

Documentation often seems forbidding because of the sheer volume of information it contains. People often convince themselves it's going to be difficult and dull before they even open it. It's up to you as the writer, therefore, to lead them through this difficulty by making challenging content comprehensible.

Engage individual readers by talking to them directly (if appropriate for the type of document you're writing) by addressing them as '*you*', rather than writing about '*the user*' or '*the customer*' or in some other impersonal manner.

Provide an introduction that sets out the context and background for what is to follow. Don't just provide information; provide an explanation, or guided tour, of your document. This will help readers to appreciate *how* and *why* you have organised your document into chapters or sections and make it less intimidating.

Writing for the Many

If writing for readers of different technical backgrounds, they will probably require different things from your document. In this case, consider whether separate (targeted) documents are more appropriate or, perhaps, a single document split into dedicated sections or chapters providing different levels of detail. Always state clearly who the intended audience is for your document, chapter or section.

Writing for the Inexperienced

Rather than '*doing the minimum*' and simply telling your readers how to use a product or service, consider whether it would be beneficial to provide guides, tutorials, examples or to educate them in the scientific, technological or business principles used.

By including such information, you help build a rapport with readers who are new to the job or not as technically savvy. This also gives them a better appreciation of *why* your product or service is superior to those of your competitors.

12. Writing for an Internal Audience

If you're writing for an internal audience, i.e. one within your own company or organisation, you may be tempted to think less about the scope, the appearance and even the accuracy of your document. But that would be a mistake.

The effectiveness of your document, not to mention your reputation, may suffer if you fail to give adequate consideration to your content, formatting and presentation. Always adopt a professional attitude to writing any document, whether internal or external. It's always an opportunity to impress.

Consider What to Include

Writing a document in haste (without proper research, analysis, or attention to detail) may be what you have been asked to do, but your boss will not be happy if it contains embarrassing omissions, inaccuracies, errors or inconsistencies.

Take time to research and think about what is '*essential*' for your document and consider what else would be '*nice-to-have*'. You can compromise on the '*nice-to-haves*', if you are pushed for time, but you must include the '*essentials*'.

In particular, when writing procedures for operating or maintaining machinery, always include any relevant warnings and cautions. The cost (personal and financial) of not doing so could be considerable.

Consider Image Quality

The quality of images and illustrations is always an issue with internal documents, since you probably don't need to meet the same exacting standards that you would for an external publication or printed document. As an inexperienced writer you may be unsure how to adjust the resolution of images obtained from dubious sources, but always check it is, at least, legible.

Consider Printing & Page Dimensions

There's always a chance someone will want to print out your document, even if that was not your intention, so be sure to set appropriate page dimensions before you begin writing.

The size of your internal document will almost always be the size used by your office photocopier (A4 for the UK and Letter or Legal for the US). This also means, if you're writing a lengthy document, you'll need to add page numbering. Once you do that you're going to need to include a contents list too.

Format and styling are perhaps not as important for an internal document but bear in mind that this can aid comprehension, retention and the overall effectiveness of your document. You'll probably be able to squeeze more text on a page and use a little less white space, unless intending to impress the board of directors.

Consider Document Management & Control

If the document is a one-off, or if it just a single sheet, you may think there's no need to identify it with a part number or issue (version/edition) number. However, think about how you're going to store this document on your computer and whether it may require updates it in the future. Is it possible that someone will spot a mistake and want it corrected and updated? How will you (or your readers) identify which is the up-to-date version?

13. Writing for an External Audience

If writing for an external audience, i.e. for people outside your office or organisation, such as customers, end-users or third parties; you need to make an extra effort to produce good documentation as your company's reputation is on the line.

Consider How You Can Add Value

If your company has designed a product that's complicated to use, difficult to install or confusing to understand; how you document it could, potentially, make it much more straightforward and comprehensible.

It's always worth spending some time thinking about the different ways you could present information. By adding value to the information you have to present, you may generate more sales, simplify an installation, clarify an operation, or reduce repair times for your company's products.

Writing for Specialists

If you're writing for engineers, developers, accountants or business professionals, you can assume a certain level of knowledge and you won't need to explain everything from first principles. You should be able to use jargon, acronyms, abbreviations and technical terms they are familiar with. Always consider, however, whether these terms need explaining, or writing in full. A little explanation, or the inclusion of a glossary of terms, might be useful to some of your readers.

Writing for the General Public

Writing for the general public is always tricky because you can't assume a level of knowledge; you can't even assume they're interested. Many user manuals and installation guides are discarded because people just don't want to read them.

There are a few things you can do to make your writing more attractive to readers:

- **Be clear.** Simplify your descriptions and instructions using fewer and shorter words to make it easier to read and remember.
- **Be personal.** Address your reader personally using "*you*" and "*your*" rather than saying "*the user can...*".
- **Be graphic.** Use illustrations or images; they really can be more helpful than long-winded descriptions.
- **Be entertaining.** An occasional humorous or personal comment can lift a dull explanation, e.g., "*Here's the legal bit. You know we have to do this, right?*"

Consider Document Management & Control

A part and issue number for your document is essential if it is to be distributed outside the company. If a customer contacts your company with a problem, you (and they) will need to know that they have the correct documentation and the up-to-date version.

When a product or service is updated with new features, the documentation also needs to be updated (up-issued). Always be clear about which product or service version your document relates to and state this on the document so your customers are in no doubt.

14. Assessing the Scope of Your Document

When you know who you're audience is, you can consider what topics need to be included in your document. Seek out other people's opinions too including your boss, any technical expert(s) and, if possible, your readers.

Your company guidelines and health and safety requirements may also affect the scope of your document. Get everyone's input you can think of and write it all down, along with your own thoughts and ideas.

Brainstorm the Required Topics

List the topics to be included in your document with no regard, at this stage, for their order or how detailed these topics will be. You can also make a list of the images/graphics that you might need to support these topics. These could include:

- Screenshots.
- Navigation diagrams.
- Overview diagrams.
- Troubleshooting flowcharts.
- Equipment illustrations.
- Engineering drawings.
- Functional diagrams.
- Front and rear views.
- Connector close-ups.
- Removal/replacement illustrations.
- Charts and graphs.
- Company logos.
- Health and safety symbols.

Identify what is essential content as well as what would be nice-to-have. Give priority to the essential topics.

Research Previous Documents

It's likely that documents, similar to the one you're writing, will already have been written. Ask around and search your company network to see if you can find any. These may be a useful guide as to what topics to include and provide a template for style and formatting. Not doing this could potentially cause problems later if there is a company standard to follow and you haven't bothered to find it.

Research Your Competitors

See if your competitors have produced something similar by visiting their website. These could also be a valuable guide as to what to include and help you anticipate the expectations of your customers. Do a better job than your competitors, and you'll please your boss, delight your customers and enhance your own reputation.

Create an Order for Your Topics

When you know what topics your document needs to cover, you can create a list of contents and a list of figures, giving you a starting point for gathering information. You can, and probably will, add to these lists and re-order them later once you have started gathering information or started writing, but for now it will serve as a first draft list of contents.

15. Structuring Your Document

When you've worked out what topics your document should contain, and have started to gather the information you need, you can organise your content to create an ordered and intuitive document.

Why is Structure Important?

Your topic sequence should make intuitive sense to your readers and encourage them to read your document from front to back. This, in turn, will help them use the product or service effectively. Keep asking yourself, *"What does the reader need to know next?"*

Readers must be able to navigate your document easily when searching for something specific; your structure can make this easy or difficult.

How to Structure Your Writing

When readers consult your document, they're usually interested in one particular aspect, such as: how to install it, how to repair it or, perhaps, how to replace a component. Other information simply gets in the way. These different aspects, often called *'categories'*, are best separated into different sections or chapters.

All your topics, corresponding to main ideas, features or components, should be clearly identified with unique headings. Introduced them, explain them and develop the detail. If writing at length on a topic, break your writing into logical, functional or practical chunks and give each a descriptive sub-heading.

Don't Overthink It

Always try to structure your document intuitively. A classic example of overthinking the structure is to place installation information at the back of a product user manual. The thinking goes like this:

"The user only needs installation information once and, when the equipment is installed, will have to skip passed the information

every time they read the manual; therefore, why not put it at the back of the document as a reference section."

While having some merit, this defies the intuitive sense of having installation information at the front (because it's the first thing a user needs to do). Hiding it away at the back means there's a chance the user won't think to look there and installation may happen without it, which could result in problems. Always go with the obvious and the intuitive.

Avoid the Information Dump

When engineers, developers, scientists and other *'detail'* people write about their own work, they often write everything they know in one place. When describing a feature, they may explain how to install and use it, describe what the LEDs do and might even offer some removal and replacement advice.

A comprehensive information dump is not useful for someone learning about a topic for the first time because it overwhelms them with information. Also, when readers are looking for something specific, it's often difficult and time-consuming to locate it if it's hidden in a mass of irrelevant description.

All documents should have an intuitive structure, even emails, to provide effective and efficient communication.

Front & Back Matter

Every document should clearly identify itself and state its purpose at the front. If the main body of the document is structured and contains headings, a list of contents should also be supplied in the front matter to enable readers to navigate to the relevant page(s).

The back of the manual is the place for reference material that is not required reading (reference tables, notes, glossary of terms, technical specification, etc.). An index may also be useful for finding keywords buried within your paragraphs.

16. Formatting Your Document

If you're told, *"It doesn't matter what it looks like"* or to *"Use default styles"*, disregard this advice. Formatting is NOT just about the appearance of your document. Investing a little time designing and formatting your document will create one that is much more effective and easier to use.

Why is Formatting Important?

The format you choose will contribute to its success (or failure):

- **Legibility** – Is text clear and suitably sized?
- **Readability** – Is text easy to read and comprehend?
- **Clarity** – Are the different elements of your content (headings, notes, warnings, etc.) distinct and identifiable?
- **Emphasis** – Is it clear why and when attributes (size, bold, italics, capitals, colour, etc.) are used, and what these mean?
- **Navigation** – Can component parts (chapters, sections, headings, tables, illustrations, etc.) be located quickly?
- **Suitability** – Is the appearance and presentation of information suitable for each topic?
- **Accessibility** – Is your content appropriately presented for your audience (people with disabilities or language issues)?
- **Consistency** – Are text and graphical elements consistently formatted throughout your document?
- **Comprehension** – Is complex and detailed information presented in the best way possible?

Styles Save You Time

It is worth learning the basics of *how* and *when* to use styles. Styles save you time by automatically formatting text of the same type (with font size, bold, italic, colour, alignment and others attributes). You simply need to label each text element (heading, paragraph, warning, etc.) with the correct style name. If you then decide to change the appearance of any text element (e.g., make a heading larger), all similarly styled elements will be automatically updated.

Styles Ensure Consistency

Using styles ensures consistency in the appearance of similar text elements. .Not using styles means formatting every heading and paragraph manually and the longer your document is, the more mistakes you will make and the longer it will take.

Lack of consistency in your text attributes undermines your document structure, confusing and frustrating your readers if they are unable to identify your text elements and their hierarchy (*"Is this a new heading, a sub-heading, or something different?"*).

Styles Generate a Table of Contents (ToC)

When you label all your headings with a style, your word processing software identifies them and extracts the text to create a contents list at a place, and in a style, of your choosing. This will save you a lot of time and ensure consistency, as opposed to manually typing a table of contents, which will be difficult to keep updated if changes are made to the document.

Are Styles Defined in Your Master Template?

If there's a company master template, this will, hopefully, have styles defined. If so, learn how to apply them. If not, or if they are insufficient for your purpose, create your own. Remember to include examples of what your styles look like and when to use them. Also remember to give your master template a part and issue number, and keep it updated.

17. Designing a Stylesheet

It needn't take long to create a set of core styles. Be mindful not to spend an excessive amount of time developing styles for every possible text variant used in your document. If variants occur only occasionally, it may be quicker to format them manually.

What Styles Do You Really Need?

Typically, you'll need about 15 or 20 styles for most technical, business or legal documents:

- **Title/Chapter** – For size and position on the page.
- **Heading1/2/3** – For heading levels, each decreasing in size or weight to show their significance.
- **Paragraph (body/normal)** – For all body text (normal paragraphs).
- **Unordered (bulleted) list** – For bulleted (perhaps indented) lists. Sub-lists may require additional styles.
- **Ordered (numbered) list** – For numbered (perhaps indented) procedural steps. Sub-procedures may require additional styles.
- **Note** – For important and noteworthy asides.
- **Caution** – For cautionary advice (damage to equipment).
- **Warning** – For warnings of danger (injury or death).
- **Tables** – A (numbered) table caption style as well as a table column heading style and a table text content style.
- **Figures** – A (numbered) figure caption style for images.
- **Header/Footer** – A smallish text for the running header and/or footer, referencing the chapter or document title.
- **Page Number** – For size and position of the automatic numbering of each page.
- **Table of Contents (TOC)** – For size, indentation and spacing of the different TOC levels, referencing the heading levels you have defined for your document.

Document Additional Formatting Rules

You'll need to specify any manual formatting rules for text, table and graphical elements that can't be defined by styles. These include table line thickness, colour and positioning; illustration line thickness, colour and shapes; callout text size, positioning and alignment, etc.

Show Examples

All your work on styles and formatting rules will be wasted if you simply define them and don't document what they are supposed to look like or when they are to be used. If you haven't one already, create a master template to document all your styles and rules, showing examples of how and when to use them.

Keep Your Template Updated

You may not (probably will not) be aware of all the situations in your document that require a defined style or formatting rule. Define as many as you can up-front and then update your master template as you encounter new situations and define new styles. Once documented, you (and others) can refer to this template to achieve consistent formatting throughout your documents.

18. Using Information Design Techniques

'*Information design*' is about designing documents that look good AND communicate effectively. Format and presentation is not just for appearances but assists the delivery, understanding and retention of information.

Treat every document as an '*information design*' task rather than just '*technical writing*' (focusing on content) or '*graphic design*' (focusing on presentation). This will help your readers to process information successfully and quickly.

Information design techniques are important to UX/UI and web designers, marketing people, technical authors, and should be considered by anyone attempting to produce a professional document.

Know Your Audience

Research your audience, and the information they require, so you don't over- or under-estimate their needs. Don't be afraid to provide additional help for those who are not up-to-speed or who are, perhaps, new to the subject.

Determine Your Objectives

Identify your purpose for writing and establish the objective(s) of your communication. Be sure you know what you're trying to achieve before you begin writing.

Select the Most Effective Medium

Examine the options you have for delivering your message (printed or online document, video, Powerpoint presentation, etc.) and choose the most effective communication medium that will support your objective(s).

Engage Your Audience

Use graphic design techniques to engage your audience, direct their attention and maximise their comprehension of the information and/or message you're communicating.

Deliver Your Message

Communicate your message in a clear, concise and compelling manner. Use repetition, if necessary to summarise the main points, highlight the takeaways or stress the essentials.

Edit, Review, Repeat

Edit and review your document before delivering it to your intended audience. Start by editing it yourself until you're confident you won't be embarrassed by any obvious mistakes. Then send it to others for expert review and managerial approval.

Test & Modify

Test the effectiveness of your document by collecting feedback from your reviewers and, if possible, a sample audience. Modify as required. You can't please all the people all the time, so *you* will have to be the final arbiter. If you run out of time, collect feedback and save it for your next issue.

Remember, you are checking for more than just spelling errors. If that's the only feedback you get from reviewers, ask them questions about how easy it was to find information, read and use. Find out what they did and didn't like, and how they think it could be improved.

19. Using Graphic Design Techniques

When creating a document, ask yourself, *"What should this type of document look like?"* Find examples to give you design ideas. Graphic elements; such as headings, paragraphs, graphics, lines, boxes, sidebars, etc., can be, coloured, re-sized, emphasised and arranged to give an intuitive body language and visual impact, which will direct the attention of your readers.

Select an Overall Style (Traditional or Modern?)

Serif fonts (those with small extensions at the end of long strokes) are recognised as a traditional, classic or establishment choice. Serifs improve readability and reading speed of long passages of text because they help to guide the eye along the line of text. They are usually, but not always, used for body text.

Non-serif fonts are simpler and more modern but can still be quite classy. They are usually, but not always, used for headings and titles. Make sure the font you choose re-enforces the message you're attempting to deliver and the impression you want to give.

Set a Mood (Dull or Vibrant?)

Colour, spacing and border size can all be adjusted to make a document appear calm or shouty. The colour scheme you use, however, may be limited by your corporate colours. Dark colours and dull shades are perceived as calmer, more sober and serious; whereas bright colours and hues appear vibrant, energetic and even frivolous.

Exhibit a Relationship (Harmony or Discord?)

A visual unity, connection or harmony between different graphic elements may be achieved by repeating colours, line thicknesses and shapes to stylistically connect them. Alternatively, a diversity, dissonance or discord may be achieved by choosing attributes that clash to clearly separate individual elements.

Establish Order (Hierarchy or Equality?)

Size, weight and boldness of colour can be used on textual or graphic elements to establish a hierarchy, importance and an intuitive order in which the elements are to be read. Careful use of these attributes will lead the eye and direct your reader's attention.

Grab & Direct Attention (Emphasis or De-emphasis?)

Highlighting important information instinctively attracts attention by making a word, a block of text or a graphic element stand out against the main body.

Create a Balance (Symmetrical or Asymmetrical?)

A balanced composition intuitively looks and feels right. It is stable and aesthetically pleasing. This is achieved by arranging design elements AND spacing so that no one area dominates. Compositional cohesiveness is controlled by weighting (size, strength and texture), positioning and distributing the elements.

Symmetrical balance is achieved when the visual weight of design elements is evenly distributed about a central or horizontal axis.

Asymmetrical balance is often less obvious, and more difficult to achieve, with the weighting of each element chosen to achieve cohesion even though elements are positioned irregularly.

20. Calculating Time-to-Completion

Whether your document is an email, a Powerpoint presentation or a user manual; don't expect to get it right first time. It will take several drafts, with the content being reviewed and approved by others prior to publication.

Will Information Gathering or Research be Required?

If you don't have immediate access to source material, you may need to spend time researching or collecting information. You may also need to arrange meetings to speak to technical experts, if the information you seek is inside their heads.

How Many Drafts Will be Required?

As a general rule, three drafts is a good number to aim for. Produce an initial document that has been written and researched by you (first draft), then reviewed by the relevant technical people (second draft) and then approved by management (final draft).

Resist requests for further drafts if several experts want to review your document. Distribute your first draft to everyone at the same time, rather than sending it to an individual reviewer for comments that are incorporated before sending to the next, as this will unnecessarily delay your document production. Incorporate all the expert comments into a second draft.

Set Review Deadlines

When you distribute a draft document, give your reviewers a deadline by which all comments are to be received; otherwise it could take a very long time. Reviewing your document will be a low priority for others, who will naturally prioritise their own work ahead of yours. Ensure your document progresses according to your timetable to ensure it is ready for the launch of the product or service. Instruct your reviewers that failure to return the draft on time will risk the delay of the product or service launch.

Devise a Documentation Plan

A basic calculation of the time required to produce your document will probably include:

1. **Information Gathering.** Gather and research the information you will need. Interview those experts who can contribute to your document.
2. **Establish Styles & Rules.** Create or obtain a template or stylesheet. This could become a mini documentation project in itself, requiring reviews and approval.
3. **First Draft.** Write (and illustrate) the first draft, typically the largest portion of your plan. Information may be missing at this stage but your reviewers may be able fill in the gaps. Make sure there are no glaring errors and you're happy to be judged on the content (because you will be).
4. **Technical Review.** First draft reviewed by Subject Matter Experts (SME) to ensure it is technically correct.
5. **Second Draft.** Incorporate all technical review comments in the second draft. You will be the arbiter of whether comments are incorporated or not.
6. **Management Review.** Second draft reviewed by management to incorporate final comments and approve the document for publishing.
7. **Final Draft - Publish.** Incorporate management review comments in the final (approved) document.

A spreadsheet or tabular/graphical plan is useful for detailing the days, weeks or months required to carry out your plan. Schedule tasks using a calendar highlighting delivery and publishing dates.

Documentation as a Component

In an ideal world, documentation should be treated as just another component part of the product being developed. In practice, this rarely happens. Always treat it as such in your planning, and integrate it, as far as you are able, with product or service development.

21. Delivering On Time

Delivering on time is crucial in any business environment. Large projects are completed only because they are organised according to a schedule, enabling teams to work in parallel and supply the constituent parts at the right time.

Make Realistic Plans

Often, unrealistic plans and schedules are produced due to the pressures of getting to market quickly or because an influential customer makes unreasonable demands for delivery. With impractical plans and unworkable schedules, deadlines are missed. This can result in plans frequently having to be updated with deadlines being moved, which disrupts all teams and departments and wastes more time as work is rescheduled.

Find Out What the (Real) Deadline Is

If someone says they need your document by a certain date, always ask, "*Why?*" Check it's a real deadline. Some people will toss a deadline at you to get you to prioritise their work over anything else you might be doing. Tell them whether it's possible (or not) or say you need time to assess and will get back to them.

Don't allow yourself to be pressured into agreeing to a deadline you know is impractical. People who invent deadlines are often in a panic. It's surprising how often *"We need it by Friday"* becomes *"Actually, it wasn't urgent after all"* the following Monday.

Plan Backwards

When creating a documentation plan, work backward from the delivery deadline or publishing date to schedule when you need to start writing. Create a realistic real-time plan that can be completed in normal work time (without evening and weekend working), allowing for holidays (especially during the summer), and with a little extra built in for unexpected issues (sickness or reviewing delays). Only then can your plan succeed. If there are unforeseen delays (there always are), you can then consider evening or weekend working to get the plan back on track.

Don't Bury Yourself in the Planning

While planning is important, don't spend too much time creating plans and periodically updating them. Your time is always better spent writing.

Schedules don't have to be, and cannot be, exact. Due to the nature of writing they will only ever be estimates. Planning what you will be writing on any particular day is futile because you can't tell in advance how long a document section will take to write (or an illustration take to produce). Spending an unwarranted amount of time creating and updating plans will inevitably delay the document.

When planning, be sure to use a tool that gives quick results and doesn't demand a high level of accuracy, or detail, that you cannot specify. That's called *'fiction'*.

It's easy to get drawn into spending excessive amounts of time planning when a popular planning software tool (you probably know the one) is the company standard. I've witnessed situations where it took a competently skilled manager an entire morning to update a plan that would have taken just 30 minutes in an Excel spreadsheet, or with a pencil and paper.

22. Delivering To-Budget

"Time is money", so the saying goes. And it's true. Once you start adding up all the time involved in creating a document, you and your boss may be in for a shock. This is another reason why companies are often reluctant to pay for professional documentation. It all stems from not considering the document as part of the product in the first place.

When you're in the business of producing widgets, your focus is on widgets and the time and cost of producing them. When the realisation occurs that documentation is required, resentment creeps in that it will be costly and put more pressure on the widget team just as they are trying to complete the project.

What Does a Document Really Cost?

It's not just your (author) time that needs to be considered but the time of other people (experts) you may to consult, the time of the document reviewers (technical and management). This is before any applicable printing or publishing costs, translation costs or packaging costs are calculated.

Can You Afford to Write this Document?

Unless you're a freelance author working to a fixed price, you probably won't have to calculate the true cost the documentation task you are about to take on. However, the fact that documentation costs time and money should needs to be accepted by everyone.

This is why many companies try to produce documentation *'on-the-cheap'* by getting their employees to write it. Of course, it will take them longer, and the end-result won't be as good but the cost of creating the document can be hidden within an existing project budget (by compelling engineers to work harder). Outsourcing the development of a circuit board, or a software module, is usually acceptable, however, because this is the primary work of an engineering company.

That said (and rant over), if you're planning to write a long document and you consider it will take too much of your time, or take you too long to complete, or require skills that you don't have, consider outsourcing to a contract or freelance technical author.

Do You Require Other Resources?

If your plan reveals that the documentation cannot be completed on time, you may need to split the task into smaller parts for several authors to work on in parallel. This will not only require a new plan but also involve extra work in overseeing these tasks.

Alternatively, you could get someone to do the illustrations, screenshots, images or some other aspect of the document for you. This will require working closely to ensure you get what you really need, which may involve more meetings or supervision time for you. The idea of doing this is to reduce your administration workload so you can get on and write. You'll need to judge carefully whether this is practical or not.

23. Delivering Your Plan

Before you start writing, get approval for your plan to ensure what you're intending to deliver will satisfy the requirement. Your plan should set out the parameters for what you will do and ensure there is no *'scope-creep'* (continually adding more topics). Your plan will identify goals and success criteria and will specify what will be delivered and who will be accountable. Having an approved plan ensures that everyone (who matters) is in agreement before work commences.

Requirement

Write a summary of the project requirement, as it has been explained to you. This is always a good place to start because it feeds back to your bosses that you have been listening and reminds them of what they said they wanted.

Project Schedule

Produce a schedule in tabular or graphical form, or both, with projected draft delivery dates, milestones, review dates, deadlines and any printing or translation activities.

Important Milestones

Be explicit about the completion date and other milestones such as first draft delivery, extracting important dates from the project schedule and specifying exactly when these will happen.

Threats, Risks & Challenges

It's a good idea to anticipate potential issues that could interfere with the implementation of your plan. At the very least, successful completion can only ever be achieved with the availability of source information, access to equipment, cooperation of staff, as well as prompt reviewing and approval.

Scope

Detail the intended scope of the document with a topic list as far as you are able at this stage. You might want to make everyone aware that (minor) changes will occur when writing commences as new information presents itself.

Structure

Provide a list of the proposed chapters, sections and main headings to give everyone a flavour of what the document will look like and how the content is to be organised. Again, this may change when writing commences.

Style & Format

State whether the document conforms to a company house-style, stylesheet or template. If there isn't one, explain why you need to create one. You'll probably find that others (in your marketing department) will agree that the company should have one.

Project Deliverables

List the deliverables of your documentation project such as draft PDFs, paper copies, master files, image files, etc. There shouldn't be any surprises or disappointments.

Applications

List the software applications and versions you'll be using to create your document. This ensures that others will be able to use and update files in the future.

Summary

A one-page summary, at the front of the plan, is useful for pulling together important key facts including requirement, cost (a quote if you are freelance), start date, completion date, and payment terms (for freelancers).

DOCUMENT DESIGN

24. Choosing the Right Tool for the Right Job

Platform

Before you choose your writing software, you'll need to consider what platform to use. Consider whether others in your company, and who may need to access your files, are using Microsoft Windows, Apple Macintosh or some other platform.

Word Processing/DTP/Page Layout Software

Find out if there are any company-wide software applications used for documentation. In most cases you will use what everyone else is using, but you may need to use specialist software. Consider the following:

- Do others need to be able to modify or update the file(s) you produce?
- Will others require specialist knowledge (of the software you intend to use)?
- Will your document be printed internally (photocopied) or externally (by a Print Shop)?
- Can the master files be printed externally by your Print Shop or will your software need to create a PDF?

- Will it be printed in black and white, or in colour? Can your software produce colour separations?
- Are you going to print (a few copies) digitally or do you need offset lithography (for hundreds/thousands of copies)?
- What size will your document be? Will it need to be printed on special paper?
- Will it require a separate printed cover?
- How will your document be delivered to your customers / readers? How will they be able to access and read it?
- Does it require translation and will your translation company be able to handle your supplied files?

Drawing/Illustration Software

If you intend to include drawings/illustrations in your document, you will need to store the original master/source files so they can be updated or modified. Do you need special illustration software or can you use the drawing tools included with your word processing software?

Photo-Editing Software

If you going to take photos, screenshots or if you will be retouching images, will you require advanced editing/retouching tools (blurring, cloning, filtering, etc.)? Will you need to spend time learning how to use this software and its tools?

Publishing & Distribution Software

If you're planning to deliver PDF documents, does your software allow you to do that? Do others within your company use a particular PDF tool or software? Will you be delivering PDF documents for reviewing and commenting or will you distribute printed versions? Do others have access to the necessary reviewing tools? Do you know how to produce a high-definition PDF for printing?

25. Designing for Print

Numbering Your Pages

If you're writing a multi-page document, it's essential you number each page, by placing a page number field in the footer. This field will automatically number each page, provided you start it off correctly. Applying a style to this field will ensure it is formatted consistently throughout your document.

If you have a significant number of preliminary pages (title page, publishing details, copyright, contents, etc.), it's usual to separate them from the main text by using Roman numerals (i, ii, iii, etc.) for page numbering. Your main text will then start from page 1 onward. Alternatively, Arabic numerals (1, 2, 3, etc.) can be used for the preliminary pages ('*prelims*') and continue for the main text to the end of the document.

Setting Your Margins & Gutter

Depending on the binding method you use, you'll need to set margins (white space) around the edge of each page to '*frame*' your content.

If you're intending to print on both sides of the paper and/or bind the document, you'll need to set a gutter. This creates additional space for binding, ensuring your text is not trapped in the fold or spoilt by hole punching.

Margin and gutter settings affect how much of the page is left for text, which in-turn affects the pagination and length of your document, so set these at the start before you do any writing.

Printing In-House

If your document is for internal use, or if you're generating only a few copies, using your company photocopier/printer may be the best option for printing. Make sure your page size is set correctly (A4 for UK, letter or legal for the US). If you're intending to bind, staple, or four-hole punch your document, ensure you've set your margins and gutter to facilitate this.

Digital Printing

If using a Print Shop to print copies digitally, you'll need to supply a suitable file (probably a PDF or DOCX). Always ensure your PDF is of high quality resolution (300 or 600dpi) for print purposes.

If you supply a DOCX file, make sure the Print Shop has same fonts as you (you may need to supply these). If you supply a PDF, this won't be necessary as fonts can be embedded. Always get a proof and check it carefully before ordering multiple copies.

The cost-per-unit of digital printing each document is the same no matter how many copies you order, so if you're intending to print hundreds you may want to consider using offset litho.

Offset Lithographic Printing

Offset lithography is used for long print runs. The larger the print run, the lower the cost-per-unit will be. A set of master plates (thin aluminium sheets) are created for your document pages and your cover artwork, which you will need to proof.

Consider creating a specification that details everything about your document (dimensions, trim size, binding method, cover printing, colour printing, binding method, etc.) so the Print Shop has all the details they need. Always inspect deliveries to be certain that what you've ordered has been delivered.

26. Designing for PDF

If your PDF is going to be both viewed and printed, it may be worthwhile creating separate PDF files for these purposes.

A print PDF creates a large file to capture text (font shapes) and images in high resolution.

A web (online viewing) PDF can be much smaller in size and of low (screen) resolution, making it more suitable for delivery and quicker to download.

Preparing A Print PDF

If preparing a PDF for printing, choose settings that create a high-resolution document (and a large file) that will result in smooth and crisp edges on printed text and images:

- Set a high (print quality) resolution (300-600 dpi). You don't want all your hard work to look pixelated or jagged.
- Any image compression should be turned off or set to a level that produces high resolution. You don't want your images, which may look acceptable on-screen, to lose their clarity when printed.
- Embed your fonts. Your printer may not have the fonts you've used, so make sure that your document will always look as you intended.
- Bookmarks are not normally required for a print PDF. No one will be reading and navigating the document online, so you can save time and reduce size by switching them off.
- You may want to use a secure password to ensure only approved people (who you have given the password to) can access your file. This also ensures the file can't be tampered with or updated without your knowledge. This happens!
- Additional settings may be required for colour, which you may need to discuss with your Print Shop.

Preparing a Web PDF

If preparing a PDF for on-screen viewing, choose settings that produce a lower-resolution document (to create as small a file as possible) that maintains on-screen clarity:

- Set a low (web quality) resolution (below 200 dpi). Check your images are still readable on-screen.
- Reduce image compression to a level that is legible on-screen. Don't assume all your images will be acceptable.
- Embed your fonts. Your viewers may not have the fonts you've used on their machine. Make sure your document always looks as you intended.
- Bookmarks are a good idea for a web PDF. This creates a set of links from your table of contents to aid with navigation. Check they have been created in the correct sequence; if you've applied heading styles incorrectly, they may not be.
- If distributing online you may want to use a secure password to ensure only approved readers (who you have given the password to) can access your file. This also ensures the file can't be tampered with or updated without your knowledge.

Colour Choices

Using colour in a web PDF is unlimited; in a print PDF it needs to be carefully considered. The colours you choose will hugely affect the cost of printing; hence, most printing still uses **black and white** (this includes grey shades).

Using a **spot-colour** (usually a single colour but could be more), perhaps for a company logo, is more expensive.

Lastly, and most expensive of all, is **full-colour** printing. Your printer will need to separate your colours into CYMK (not RGB). Some word-processing applications (Microsoft Word included) do not allow you to separate colours in this way; hence you may decide you need a different software application (Adobe InDesign, perhaps).

27. Designing for Help

Being concise is paramount when writing help text. This textual (possibly graphical) information and instruction needs to be minimal because your readers just want to get on and use their new software.

Preparing Your Help Document

While you can utilise a software user manual as source information for your help file, you shouldn't simply cut and paste this content without careful consideration.

Here are some general guidelines to producing good help text:

- **Provide concise topics with headings.** Your help file should comprise short, easy-to-read paragraphs with clear and unique topic headings.

- **Break up long passages of text.** Lengthy paragraphs and descriptions extracted from the user manual should be broken up into chunks. Nobody reads lengthy help text.

- **Create easy-to-scan topics.** Use well-chosen topic titles that answer questions your readers are asking. These are essential to helping them find the information they seek.

- **Arrange topics logically and sequentially.** A flowing series of topics will help your readers to appreciate the functional flow or operation of your product.

- **Write step-by-step instructions.** Edit your instructions brutally to minimise the number of words used. The less screen space they take up, the better.

- **Use small images and cropped screenshots.** Using images of software icons, menus and screens is a convenient way to convey information quickly and reassure your readers that they are selecting and doing the right thing.
- **Write plenty of "*How to...*" topics** (even if you don't use those actual words). Remember to answer your readers' questions: "*How do I select...*", "*Where can I find...*", "*Why has this happened?*"
- **State the reason (why), then the instruction (how).** Write in the present tense, unless there's a compelling reason not to. This uses fewer words, sets the context and is easy to comprehend, e.g., "*To turn off the unit, press the red button*".

Check the Links

Check which help topic is displayed when you press the Help button when using the software? This is called '*context-sensitive help*'. The topic displayed should depend on which screen or function is being used at the time.

To enable this, unique IDs (identifiers) must be assigned to your individual help topics. These IDs must then be inserted into the software code of the application to provide the connection between the two. Then, when the Help button or icon is pressed, the correct help topic is displayed. Speak to your software developers to ensure IDs are incorporated in their code.

Help is Part of the Product

When the software about which you are writing is updated, check to see if the help text is also affected. This will almost certainly be the case if new features have been added or if existing features have been modified or deleted.

28. Designing for Presentation

Think of each slide of a Powerpoint presentation as being a poster. How it looks is just as important as how it reads if it is to be understood and remembered.

Start with a Question

Why are we all here? What's the objective or goal? Point or tease the direction your presentation will take.

Use Headlines, Not Headings

Think like a journalist. Write emotive headings (*'How Much Will this Cost Us?'*) that target your readers, rather than merely categorising the information for your benefit (*'Cost Calculations'*).

Use Font Restraint

"Words have meaning, fonts have feeling". Make sure the fonts you use complement your message. Choose a typeface to set an appropriate look-and-feel. Don't use lots of different font types on the same slide and don't choose unsuitable fonts (i.e. jokey or flamboyant fonts for serious business). Use large fonts to shout your message and grab attention.

Use Colour Restraint

It can be a good idea to initially work in black and white (black text on white background, or vice-versa). Contrasting tones have impact. Adding colour at the end, sets the mood (optimistic, dramatic, demure, formal, polished, relaxed, etc.).

Keep Your Text Tight

Use short sentences, strong verbs and remove unnecessary words to keep your content clear and easy to understand. Think of your words as a prose poem; every word should count.

Use the Power of Three

'*Three*' is always more effective, satisfying, and memorable than other numbers. Have at least three slides, sections or reasons, such as: past, present and future; or problem, solution, and next steps.

Avoid Death by Bullet Point

People love a bulleted list but they quickly become bored when overused, so use them sparingly and to good effect. Use a diagram, rather than a bulleted list, to demonstrate a relationship or pattern between items.

Illustrate, Don't Decorate

Have good reasons for including images, illustrations and tables. Add callouts for further description, opinion or explanation.

Use a Different Page Layout for Each Slide

Make each slide unique and memorable. Using the same format for every slide is boring and unmemorable. Challenge your creativity and design skills.

Finish Strongly & With Action

Finish with a call-to-action or takeaway. What are the next steps? What can we do? How can I make a difference?

29. Designing for Translation

Count the Cost of Your Words

Translators charge by-the-word, so it literally '*pays*' to edit your content, condense your thoughts, and discard unnecessary words in order to minimise the cost.

Translators Must Speak it Like a Native

A translator needs to be a native speaker (of the language) and may require a technical or scientific background if they're to correctly translate your complex terms and concepts. A non-native, or non-technical, translator could unintentionally misunderstand your carefully chosen words. Always confirm the background of the translator before handing over your document.

Translators Don't Do Formatting

The translator must be familiar with the application you've written your document in (such as Word), because they will take your file and overwrite it, replacing English words with translated ones. They don't need to understand your styles and formatting.

Secondary staff may be used for checking the formatting your document (you may pay for this service) but you will still need to allow time to check the translated document when it is returned to you. Under no circumstances allow a translation to be printed and delivered without checking it first.

Leave Enough Room

The number of words in a foreign language almost always exceeds the English version, since English is itself quite concise.

Be prepared for headings to run over onto two (or more) lines, where previously they was only one. Don't be surprised when your carefully arranged pagination is ruined (unless you've allowed acres of white space for it to run in to).

Check Your Images

If you have images, illustrations or screenshots with callouts, you'll need to supply the original illustration files to the translator. Check they've been translated and inserted back into your text document correctly.

The length of translated callouts will probably exceed the English ones, resulting in words being scattered untidily over your original diagram. You will want to re-align and position them more neatly, in keeping with your formatting rules.

Proof the Translated Document

When the translation has been completed and delivered back to you, you'll need to verify that the translated text is accurate (by finding someone in your company you can trust to read it) and that the correct styles and formatting has not been lost or interfered with (this happens a lot). You'll also need to check that the table of contents, cross-references and index entries have been updated correctly.

Often the time required to proof read and correct a translator's work is overlooked in a documentation plan and it can be considerable. Don't expect the translator to hand you back perfectly translated and designed documents. It's a long job, especially when translating into multiple languages.

INFORMATION GATHERING

30. Collecting Source Information

When you know what topics you're going to write about you can begin researching and collecting source information from which you will extract (and rewrite) content for your document.

Access to Source Documents

Obtain access to files and directories and get copies of documents, videos, presentations, drawings, and anything else that may be useful. If this is a large amount of information you may need to create a filing/storage system to enable you to retrieve specific information as you need it.

If you're gathering information from electronic documents, use highlighting or commenting features to keep track of those sections you used in your content and those you did not. By marking up these documents you will save time and reliance on your memory if you have lots of source documents to read.

Access to People

If you've been asked to write something about which you're not an expert, you'll need to find out who the Subject Matter Expert (SME) is and whether they're willing to chat with you, to contribute by writing something or are happy to dig-out information for you.

If they're unwilling to help, speak to their line manager who will likely have a broader view of what's important to the company. Once your expert is given an instruction to assist you, they should be more cooperative.

Always prepare questions, requests and meetings to cause the least amount of interruption to your expert. These are valuable people and have important work to do. This might involve writing a detailed email request for information that they can reply to either electronically or in person at their convenience.

Access to Equipment

Ideally, if you're documenting a piece of equipment, you will usually need access to it. This can be difficult, however, as the equipment is often still in development or being tested. Do what you must to get the information you need.

If you're documenting a piece of equipment, an assembly line or some other physical system, you'll probably need access to it while it is still in development to discover how it works, take photos or capture screenshots. You may also require the assistance of an expert to explain what you're looking at and how it operates. Again, such meetings should be arranged at their convenience.

Always gather as much information as possible while you have access to the equipment. Capturing everything in one go minimises disruption to the development team. However, if you discover gaps in your information, or require additional detail later on, you may need to plan another visit. If the equipment is still in development when you gather your information, screenshots or photos, you may need to update it nearer the completion date in order to capture any last minute changes in design.

31. Asking for Input

What (Exactly) Do You Need to Know?

When asking experts for information, the more specific your questions or request, the more likely it is that you will receive helpful answer(s). Avoid being vague. Do some research beforehand in order to ask better questions.

Is this the Right Person to Ask?

Make sure you ask the right person for information. Are they the expert on this topic or an authority on the matter? Should you be speaking to their boss, or their assistant?

Is there's an Alternative Source?

Do you really need to interrupt this person or could you obtain the information from another source; the internet or a book, perhaps?

Is it the Best Way to Ask?

Are your questions something best discussed in person, or could you simply write a detailed email or make a phone call? Do you have a long list of questions or do you just want an overview to get an appreciation of what they are doing?

Is it Necessary?

Are you sure the information you're asking for is necessary for your document? Can you manage without it or is it essential for your progress?

Is it the Right Time?

Do you need information right now? If the information you're after is likely to be modified or updated, could you simply raise the question in your submitted draft document for them to answer when the design is more established.

How Can You Minimise the Interruption?

Have you adequately prepared for a meeting or interaction? Do you have a list of questions you need answers to? Have you sent them this list, so they can attend your meeting with answers? Could you have done this interaction via email?

Where Will You Meet?

Do you need a formal meeting room? Are you going to interview your expert at their desk or at the office canteen? Where would be more convenient?

How You Will Record the Information?

Are you expecting your expert to provide documents or are you going to take written notes? If so, can you write fast enough? An audio recording may help save time and be more accurate but make sure you have their permission.

When Will You Review the Received Information?

Have you set aside time after your meeting to examine the information you've collected, record details you can remember and come up with new thoughts or follow-on questions. If you leave it too long, you'll forget what was discussed.

DOCUMENT WRITING

32. Is Your English Good-Enough?

Be an Effective Writer

If you believe your standard of English isn't good, don't worry; it needn't be a barrier to you becoming an effective writer. If you're interested in being a writer, simply keep making the effort to improve. Get yourself a notebook and write down the things you learn or need to remember. And keep practicing.

Use the Tools of the Trade

Always use a **spellchecker** or **dictionary**. If your vocabulary isn't extensive, use a **thesaurus**. If you can't name the different parts of a sentence, use a **grammar checker**. Not knowing these things doesn't stop you from speaking the language. We all absorb grammatical principles by learning what sounds right in conversation and by reading.

Add Value to Information

What matters most in writing, is structuring your thoughts and clarifying your ideas. Your aim is to enable your readers to assimilate information more effectively and efficiently than you did. Transforming hours of research into a few comprehensible and enlightening paragraphs adds value by making complex information simpler to understand, utilise and memorise.

Remember, you're not trying to make a feature of your writing. A good writer fades into the background so that readers don't notice the words you use but simply absorb their meaning.

Make an Effort

What matters most in writing is adopting a professional attitude. This means making an effort, doing the research, using the tools, thinking about what you're doing, analysing why you're doing it that way. and frequently asking yourself how it can be improved.

Be Concise

Always use simple, everyday words where possible. Don't attempt to impress your readers with your vocabulary or with technical and business jargon. Sometimes, however, using jargon, technical terms, acronyms, etc., will be appropriate when delivering complex information to the right audience. You must be the judge.

Be Clear

Don't make your words a chore to read by being overly long. Break up long paragraphs, if it makes sense to do so, to make information easier to digest. Give thought to how your passages of text look on the page. Are they imposing or inviting?

Be Compelling

Engagement with your readers is everything. There's no point writing content that will bore, lose or defeat them. Strive to make your content appealing. Include nuggets, facts, details or asides that surprise and delight. If your content is, by nature, a little dull, can you make it easier to get through by skilful use of structure and format, or by breaking up long passages into more manageable chunks?

33. Thinking of the Writer

It's All Obvious, Isn't It?

Generally, engineers and software developers are the worst possible people to write about their products and services. There's good reason for this.

It's likely these technical or scientific experts have been focused for many weeks on researching and developing and they tend to forget or downplay how much they have learned in that time.

After deep immersion into their subject, they often say things are '*obvious*' or '*intuitive*' when, in fact, they are nothing of the sort. As experts in their field they are no longer able to stand back and see their subject from the standpoint of the inexperienced.

Understanding Your Role

Your role, as a communicator, is to translate the technical and complex knowledge of the expert into clear and concise language that is understandable by the inexperienced reader.

Be mindful that things may not be obvious or intuitive to them. Don't be afraid of criticism for '*patronising*' your readers or '*stating the bleeding obvious*'. Someone, somewhere will probably be glad of it.

Explain Jargon, Acronyms & Abbreviations

When it comes to describing technical, scientific or business detail; your audience expects you to write in language they understand and commonly use. Making certain your readers can understand what you are writing about is, obviously, of paramount importance.

Jargon (e.g. key metrics), initialisms (e.g. SMS) and acronyms (e.g. PIN) are probably in common usage throughout your company or industry, but can you assume that your audience knows what they mean?

Minimise jargon where possible and write out all abbreviations in full the first time they are used; thereafter, use the accepted initialism or acronym. There are, of course, exceptions to this general rule.

In my experience there are always people who don't know what abbreviations stand for. Usually they have worked in the company for some time and have heard, and even used, the abbreviation, but have no clue what it stands for.

Explain Technical and Business Terms

If you're writing a technical or business document, you probably won't be able to avoid using some complex (industry-wide) technical or business terms that only an insider would know.

Consider including a glossary of terms and abbreviations to the beginning or end of your document, to the enable the uninitiated to understand and join in the discussion.

Research abbreviations and terms; ask the experts, look online or in textbooks. Again, you're doing the work so your readers don't have to and, thereby, adding value to your writing.

34. Thinking of the Reader

Who Are They?

There's no point writing anything until you know who your readers are. The topics your document covers, the level of detail you provide and the methods you use to present that information all require an understanding of your readers' needs.

How much do your readers already know? What technical and/or business background do they have? What information do they want? Why will they need this information? Why will they read it?

Don't overthink it; just capture everything you did!

How Much Do They Know?

Will your readers have some familiarity with what you're writing about or will this all be new to them? Can you safely assume they have some knowledge or must you explain everything?

What is Their Background?

Target your document to your audience by writing at their technical and/or business level. For instance, a manager or supervisor may need a high-level (less-technical) functional detail, an end-user may need basic operator instructions and simple fault-finding advice, and a service engineer will probably need low-level (highly-technical) explanations and detailed maintenance information.

What Do They Want?

Deliver the essential information your readers expect and need. It may also be worth your while to include information they didn't know they needed but were so glad you did. Give them compelling reasons to keep reading your document by adding value and providing useful extras.

Why Will They Need It?

Think about the benefits (to your readers) your document could provide, such as:

- Helping them acquire new knowledge.
- Helping them see things in a new perspective.
- Helping them to understand background context or principles.
- Making complex detail easy to understand.
- Teaching them new skills or techniques.
- Helping them to do their job better.
- Saving them time.
- Saving them the trouble of looking elsewhere.
- Providing advice and quick fixes when things go wrong.

Why Will They Read It?

Make your document compelling by ensuring it is relevant, targeted to your intended audience and adds value to the information it presents. Convince your readers that it's better to read your document than not.

35. Starting Writing

Find Somewhere Quiet

If, like me, finding the right words and the flow requires real effort, you probably need a quiet environment to do your best work. Writing requires my whole attention; I need peace and quiet with no interference, background noise or music.

Writing in an office with conversations, phone calls and other comings-and-goings is distracting and disturbs concentration. Research proves that productivity is reduced for the majority of people when working in an open-plan environment, and yet most offices today are like this. Working in a coffee shop is just as bad.

I've found I do my best work at home in a quiet room, hence, I've been self-employed for over twenty years. My concentration and productivity increases tremendously if I can work for long periods without interruption. The problem then becomes one of making sure I take frequent breaks to keep me fresh.

Start at the Beginning

Writing an introduction or an overview (or both) at the beginning of a document enables you to review what you currently know about the subject and to discover the '*holes*' in your knowledge.

An overview gets things straight in your head and gives you (and your readers) the big picture or sets the context for the detail to follow.

Don't worry if you are unable to complete the introduction or overview at this stage, you probably don't yet have the knowledge or understanding. This will occur as you write the main body. For now, just write all you can and come back to it later when you have reached the end of the document and learned much more.

The Landing Page

Grip your readers from the start. Make sure they know they're reading the right document and it covers the subject they are interested in and contains the information they're looking for.

Advertise the benefits of it (*'By the end of this document you will know how to do this and that...'*) and lead them to explore the main body in search of detail.

Think of the introduction in the same way as a landing page for a website; it has to perform several jobs:

- Be attractive and appealing.
- Orientate your readers by providing context.
- Contain significant and appropriate content.
- Contain sufficient technical detail.
- Entice your readers to delve deeper.
- Direct your readers to the information they need.
- Reassure your readers that it's worth an investment of their time and effort.

36. Crafting Your First Draft

Writing Is a Craft

Writing is not something you can '*do*' or '*not do*', although it can seem that way in the beginning. As with other crafts, the more we practice, the better we get. From the perspective of the craftsperson, the initial goal (of being an artist, musician, cook, potter, or writer) is never truly attained or finished; there is always something more to learn and improve. They (we) are perpetual students. Good writers become '*good*' because they have spent many hours practicing and developing their craft; and they continue to do so.

Start by Copying

Good writing starts with attentive reading. Find examples you like and would like to imitate. Find a voice in your head that sounds authoritative, informative, flowing and accessible. Perhaps that voice won't be your own at first but someone's whose work you admire. Use it, and soon you'll be churning out pages you consider to be '*half-decent*'.

Encourage the Flow

Encourage your thoughts and ideas to flow onto the page. Try not to interrupt the process too much even if your writing is a bit of a jumble at first. When you get to the end of a paragraph, read it back and improve it, condense it, remove superfluous words. Then move on to the next to keep the thoughts coming. You will edit the whole draft document later, when you've reached the end.

Write, Review, Repeat

Good writing is written, edited, re-written, reviewed by colleagues, is set aside for a short time, proof-read and edited again with a fresh mind. So discard any belief you may have had that anyone can write acceptably at the first attempt. It has to be crafted.

In Joe Moran's book *'First You Write a Sentence'*, he says:

"Writing allows mediocre people who are patient and industrious to revise their stupidity and edit themselves into something like intelligence."

This applies to most writers (including me).

Take Your Time to Get Your Message Right

Former President and CEO of Amazon Jeff Bezos' advice for great writing applies to everything from writing emails to writing books, he says:

"Research and recognize what 'better' looks like and set realistic expectations for how much work is involved in achieving high standards."

In short, don't *'dash-off'* anything, ever.

Look for Examples

Find out if there's a company house style or template you should be using or that you can adapt, or improve, before you start writing your document. It's also worth doing some research to see if any similar documents have been written previously that are good examples to follow or bad examples to avoid.

37. Choosing the Right Language

Getting the language right may be difficult if you've no experience of formal writing. It has to engage your readers without being over-bearing, be personal without being overly chatty, be business-like without being boring or officious. Look at examples of similar documents to see how they have been written. Consider your options and choose a '*voice*' that suits your purpose.

A method I like to use is to imagine an actor or broadcaster, whose communication skills I admire, reading my words to see if it sounds right coming out of their mouths. This often brings to light the changes I need to make.

Spoken or Written?

It's important to appreciate the difference between spoken and written language.

Spoken language should not be used for written documents. It's often used, however, because it's spontaneous and requires less thinking. Hastily chosen and abbreviated words can make the message unintelligible. The shortcuts we use in spoken language can lead to misinterpretation when incorporated into a written medium.

Written language is (or should be) carefully constructed. It takes no shortcuts or deviations and uses complete sentences with carefully considered grammar and punctuation, the rules of which are there precisely to avoid confusion and misunderstanding.

Formal or Informal?

In general, written English is more formal than spoken English, but the degree of formality required for a document depends on the situation and the audience. When writing, you will need to make decisions about the rules you are going to adopt. To ensure you use them consistently, write them down in your style and formatting guide.

Personal or Impersonal?

The level of formality you use needs careful consideration. Being too informal could give the impression of being not serious or business-like.

- **Level 0 – Impersonal.** Documents can be completely impersonal, and therefore entirely formal, by referring to the customer or the reader as '*the reader*', '*the user*', '*the contractor*' or similar. This maintains distance between the writer (the company) and the audience. It indicates that you do not know, or wish to develop, a personal relationship. It's often the method used in contracts, agreements, and other business, legal or academic documents.

- **Level 1 – Personal.** Introducing the second-person pronoun '*you*' and '*your*', instead of '*the user*' or '*the user's*' breaks the barrier between the writer and the reader. It's often used in product user manuals or installation guides. It sends a message that a personal relationship has been established. Your reader will intuitively feel like they are being spoken to and involved.

- **Level 2 – Casual.** This level of informality introduces those contractions used in informal speech. This demonstrates a level of friendliness that you might use in a book (like this one), a website or a personal email. It actually requires more punctuation than formally written text by shortening words and discarding characters. It uses expressions such as: you're (you are), you'll (you will), you'd (you would), could've (could have), can't (cannot), it'll (it will), it's (it is), it'd (it would), won't (will not), don't (do not), let's (let us), etc.

- **Level 3 – Down with the Kids.** More contractions, abbreviations, slang and verbal expressions are the preserve of fiction. In this sort of writing, the writer is replicating actual speech (obvs!).

38. Writing Captivating Headings

Using Title Case (Correctly)

Title case is widely used in headings but the rules are not universally standardised. You will, therefore, need to document how you are going to implement it in your style guide. A simple set of rules (used in this book) is outlined below.

When using title case, all words (nouns, pronouns, verbs, adjectives, adverbs) are capitalised, except for:

- Articles (a, an, the, this, that)
- Prepositions (in, into, of, with, without, under, over, before, after, towards, between)
- Conjunctions (and, but, for, or).
- Some others (to, from, by, as)

NOTE: The first and last word should always be capitalised, even if it's one of the exceptions listed above.

Using Initial Caps

An easier way to write headings is to use initial capitals on ALL words. This has the advantage that it can usually be set as a style in your word processing software, so it will occur automatically. It doesn't always look right but will ensure you are consistent.

Using ALL CAPS

Using all capitals can be SHOUTY but does distinguish, even more clearly, what is a heading and what is body text. Again, this can be incorporated into a style to be applied automatically.

Using sentence case

Using sentence case for headings looks trendy but can lead to confusion about what is a heading and what is body text, especially if the heading is followed by a short sentence.

Captivate & Control by Asking Questions

A question, especially if it is one your readers are keen to find the answer to, can make an attention-grabbing heading. A question can get them to focus by making them think. A series of questions, carefully prepared, can engage their curiosity, guide them down a path and encourage them to delve deeper.

Spice-Up Your Headings - Write Headlines

You should consider using this journalistic device, where appropriate, for engaging your readers with emotive and thought-provoking headlines ("*Why the Power Supply Won't Blow Up*"). A simply descriptive heading merely categorises information and is often written for your, not your readers', benefit.

Have Distinctive Levels & Styles

Ensure your heading levels stand out from your body text and are sufficiently different from each other so they can be identified by scanning a page. To achieve this, carefully select their size (largest = highest level), their emphasis (bold or italics) and their colour (lighter tones fade into the background and are less prominent).

Use Ampersand (&) and Punctuation Appropriately

The ampersand is an informal shortcut (for '*and*') and therefore NOT normally used in formal documents or within text, being considered slang. It can be used in headings and titles that are less formal (I've used it throughout this book).

Full-stops are NOT normally used at the end of headings. But question marks and exclamation marks are used where a heading demands it.

39. Choosing the Right Words

Don't Write to Impress

It's always tempting to use big words. As a writer you want to convince your readers that you're a worthy author. Remember, you're NOT writing to impress, or even be noticed, you're writing to distribute information and help others to understand.

If you can use a simpler word – you should. Using straightforward language ensures everyone is included. Using the same words all the time can, however, be boring, so use a thesaurus to find some (simple) alternatives (synonyms).

Keep Jargon & Technical Terms to a Minimum

In technical, scientific or business writing, it's often impossible to avoid using technical terms and industry-wide jargon. While you may think you know your readers, you have to allow for a degree of inaccuracy in your estimation. Assuming your readers know what you know is often a mistake.

Your readers will never have *exactly* the same knowledge or experience as you. Be mindful of what you've learned and how long you've been immersed in the subject. Strive to write using words anyone could understand.

Use Anglo-Saxon (Verbs) over Norman (Nouns)

Formal writing can be exceedingly boring. Why is this?

Verbs are action words; they are naturally dynamic. They offer a subjective vision of the world, speaking in terms of '*being*' and '*doing*'. They tell us what's happening now, what happened previously and what will happen in the future. The Anglo-Saxon language gave us lots of verbs at a time when people enjoyed being alive and free without the need to focus on the things they owned. Use a verb and the reader visualises an action or process. Using more verbs will captivate your reader.

Nouns, on the other hand, are naturally static. They label the objects around us (concrete nouns) and things that can't be touched (abstract nouns).They offer an objective view of the world, speaking in terms of things. The Norman (French) language introduced nouns to do with land grabbing, asset ownership and legal documents (the result of invasion in 1066). Sentences are re-structured to introduce nouns where verbs should be. Use a noun and the reader's mind focuses on a static object. Even today, inserting more nouns into your sentences is considered a loftier, classier or more formal way of speaking. Using fewer nouns will stop you from boring your reader (and restrain your ego).

Choosing verbs over nouns will make your sentences shorter, more direct and easier to understand. I frequently catch myself creating noun-heavy sentences where verbs would be more effective. "*Have a read of this document*", turns the verb '*read*' into a noun (a thing) rather than saying simply, "*Read this document*". Have a think about this yourself (Oh no, I did it again). I mean, of course, "*Think about it*".

40. Choosing Concise Words & Phrases

Replacing Stock Phrases

Many stock (i.e. clichéd) phrases can (and should) be replaced to make sentences concise and easier to read.

Wordy	Concise
in order that/to	so/to
so that we can	to
due to the fact that	because
during the course of	during
in the event that	if
regardless of the fact that	although
for the simple reason that	because
at this point in time	then
with the exception that	except
a number of	some, many

Remove Redundant Words

Many words and phrases can (and should) be removed altogether because they are weak and unnecessary.

Weak Words	More Weak Words
very	really
I think that...	so
the areas of	honestly
in my opinion	amazing
for all intents and purposes	always
needless to say	absolutely
that	always
there is/are	never
literally	just
basically	actually

Avoid Business Jargon

Avoid '*office jargon*' or '*management speak*', if you want to simplify and clarify your writing.

Jargon to Avoid	More Jargon to Avoid
going forward	on the same page
thinking outside the box	get the ball rolling
blue sky thinking	low-hanging fruit
leverage (as a verb)	helicopter view
state-of-the-art	vertical
price point	close of play
feedback (as a verb)	ping me (email me)
touch base	remuneration
game-changing	synergy
bandwidth	dialogue (as a verb)

Choose Words with a Singular or Specific Meaning

Some words have multiple meanings and might confuse your readers, causing them to re-read sentences to comprehend their intended meaning. If there's a less-confusing or more-specific word, use it.

Be precise with your language but don't get too hung-up on finding the '*perfect*' word when a '*better*' one will improve understanding.

41. Writing Engaging Sentences

Always Start with the Big Picture

Research proves that sentences are easier to comprehend when we place the most important item first, followed by a drilling-down into the detail. This gives us the context, explaining how the detail fits into the big-picture. It seems we all need the hook to hang it on in order to comprehend and remember facts.

Use Short Sentences

A good sentence gives order and clarity to your thoughts. Don't add surplus words to try to make things clearer, try instead to use better words. Readers always prefers fewer, well-chosen words so an entire thought or idea can be held in memory. If further clarification is needed, add another sentence.

Examine every sentence you write to see if it can be written in fewer words (less than 25 is good), or if it can be split into two, or more, sentences. However, don't use this rule rigidly; alternating short and long sentences can bring your writing to life by surprising and stimulating your readers.

Adverbs, Adjectives & Cliches

Formal and business writing generally uses a minimal number of adverbs and adjectives. Although marketing people tend to get carried away when describing their innovative, state-of-the-art, world-leading, best-in-class, award-winning solutions (are we gagging yet?). Naturally, if you're writing a document that's not selling anybody anything, then all that surplus and emotive hype should be cut from your content.

Avoid trite and tired clichés, like 'state-of-the-art', and 'blue-sky thinking', unless of course you're writing for an audience who appreciate that sort of thing.

Write in the Present Tense

It's easy to accidentally write in a mix of tenses, especially when writing about a sequence of events. This can make it more difficult for your readers to comprehend. Always write in the present tense, unless deliberately talking about something that happened in the past or will happen in the future.

Active or Passive Voice?

Active voice = good, passive voice = bad, right? Actually, it's horses for courses, especially in professional writing.

In an active sentence, the word order is straightforward and simple: the subject of the sentence performs an action (the verb), and the object receives it, e.g.:

'*This document describes the product*'.

Active voice is direct, straightforward and easier to comprehend because it is logically sequenced. It also uses fewer words. Try to use the active voice unless there are good reasons not to, as this will make your writing clearer and more concise.

In a passive sentence, the word order is reversed: the subject of the sentence receives the action and the object performs it, e.g.:

'*The product is described by this document*'.

Passive voice is a useful device used in official (and officious) writing, in signage and in threatening letters because reduces or avoids responsibility or blame for delivering the message. The object is removed entirely – seeming saying, "*It's just one of those things*", e.g. "*Dogs are not allowed*", rather than actively saying, "*We do not allow dogs*". There are times when the passive voice is useful and necessary, especially when you've been asked to write on someone else's, or a company's, behalf. Consequently, it has its uses in legal, academic, and business writing.

Try rewriting in the active voice to see if it makes your sentence more personal and, more importantly, more comprehensible.

42. Writing Purposeful Paragraphs

New Paragraph, New Subject

Every paragraph should present a new subject, aspect or idea concerning the topic about which you're writing. Several paragraphs may be required to explain the topic, and all its aspects, fully.

Each paragraph should have a relationship with the preceding one and the one following and, therefore, have a rightful place within your topic content, often called '*flow*'. If you start a new topic or a new subject, the relationship is broken and you'll need to start a new paragraph.

Connect the Sentences

Within each paragraph you need to tell the '*story*' of the subject. This will guide your reader from a beginning point, which usually describes something they know, to an end-point, which explains something they don't.

A complex subject may require several sentences within the same paragraph to explain it completely. New information should unfold naturally and extend the framework of information in a functional, logical, hierarchical or sequential manner, as appropriate.

Use Short Paragraphs

Short paragraphs make books easier to read, websites easier to digest and information easier to absorb. Examine every paragraph you write to see if it can be broken into separate topics or subjects (perhaps with some re-writing).

Use Headings to Sign-Post Your Paragraphs

Using headings and sub-headings gives your content structure by identifying the topic or subject your paragraphs describe and by specifying how they relate to each other (a hierarchy of features, perhaps). When your content has structure, it is easier for your readers to place things in context and understand the product or service.

Headings are also essential for finding topics in a long document. Scanning through the document to find something you previously read can be a pain unless there are meaningful and identifiable headings that can lead you directly to what you want to find.

Use Bullets Sparingly

Bullet-points are an effective way to present options (an itemised list) and break up what would otherwise be a long descriptive paragraph.

A bulleted list can often be enhanced by including pseudo-headings (in bold) to capture the attention of the reader. Typical examples are for switches on a piece of equipment or software buttons on a web page, which highlight the switch or button name followed by the description:

- **I/O** – Switches the coffee machine on/off.
- **STOP** – Removes power from the coffee machine in an emergency.
- **AMERICANO** – Outputs hot coffee over your trousers unless you place a cup under the output nozzle.

43. Writing Effective Instructions

Writing procedures (or instructions), often called 'Instructional Design', amounts to telling someone how to perform a particular task such as installing equipment, operating machinery, performing maintenance, etc. They may be one-time or frequently used procedures, providing directions for completing the task.

Procedures do not normally teach background skills, explain reasoning or impart supplementary knowledge, as this would obscure the instructions with more words. If further description or explanation is required, separate it out in another section or separate heading.

Be Clear and Specific

Always specify clearly, in the introduction to the procedure, what the procedure is for, i.e. what will be achieved by doing it. This will give your readers confidence that they are doing the right thing and prevent them performing irrelevant or incorrect tasks.

Use Numbered Steps

A procedure should be broken down into a series of steps, with each step performing a single actionable task. In this way even a lengthy or complicated procedure may be successfully carried out.

Numbering also helps your readers quickly return to their place in the procedure after looking away to complete each step. The form of words you use will depend on who your audience is and their technical or business background.

Write Simply & Concisely

Write each step of your procedure in as few words as is necessary to describe the task to be performed for your intended audience. Use the simplest and best words you can to ensure your instructions are clear, comprehensible and memorable. Take care not to be too terse, which could lead to misinterpretation.

Check Your Accuracy

Writing inaccurate instructions will result in your readers not performing tasks correctly, which could lead to delays or mistakes in installation, damage to equipment, incorrect operation or maintenance, and angry calls to customer support. Checking, editing and testing your procedures is vital.

Their Lives in Your Hands

Failing to include appropriate warnings and cautions PRIOR TO each step of your procedure could result in damage to equipment, personal injury or, potentially, even death; for which you and your company could be held liable.

It's no use telling your readers to *'remember to unplug the equipment first'* after they have completed your procedure, or assuming that your readers will know that mains ac power terminals are exposed when they remove an equipment casing.

Whilst some choose to place health and safety advice, warnings and cautions together at the beginning of a technical document, it is more useful to write any, and all, warnings and cautions prior to the relevant step in the procedure where it is needed, even if this means repeating the same information in multiple places.

44. Writing Training Materials

Providing training is also a form of *'Instructional Design'*. Often called *'learning and development'*, the purpose of such training is to teach the skills or impart the knowledge required to perform a task or take on a new role or responsibility.

Analyse the Requirement

Before writing anything, it's important you understand the purpose of the training and your audience. This ensures you deliver appropriate and effective training.

Define Your Objectives, Outcomes & Criteria

Be clear about your aims (what is to be achieved), define the learning outcomes (what knowledge and skills are to be acquire) and identify assessment criteria (how learning outcomes are to be measured or assessed).

Choose an Effective Method

Does the subject matter dictate whether a passive method should be used (just reading, listening or watching) or an active one (involving tasks, exercises or experiments)?

Consider whether self-directed study, attending classroom or online lectures, or holding an interactive group workshop is appropriate.

Select an Appropriate Medium

Select the most effective and appropriate medium for delivering your training. Is it better to provide a document or use some other medium (video, podcast, help project, software application, etc.)?

Also consider whether your trainees will require a reminder, a summary, a quick reference card or similar, when training has been completed and they have returned to their workplace.

Consider the Timescale and Pace of Your Delivery

The timescale for the delivery of your training course will depend on how much you have to communicate and how detailed the information is. Consider the pace of your delivery from the perspective of your students. Don't overwhelm them with an information dump (too quick) nor bore them with too much preamble (too slow). Break it up into manageable chunks. Information must be relayed at a pace they can absorb and comprehend. This will depend on their technical or business background and their aptitude.

Will this be a single event, a series of training sessions, an open-ended course of self-directed study or some other option?

Deliver Engaging Content

In addition to transferring knowledge through words and diagrams, instructional design provides an opportunity to be creative with your documentation and delivery techniques. Consider what tasks (tutorials, exercises, quizzes, etc.) and techniques (multimedia, storytelling or gamification, where the reader can win points, badges, etc.) might be appropriate.

Evaluate Your Training

Always assess the effectiveness of your training. How many trainees passed the course? Were they engaged by the training? Did they ask meaningful questions? How will they use the information and skills in their workplace? How could the training be improved?

Ask your trainees (and your trainer) for feedback. Include a feedback form at the end of your documentation. Analyse their feedback and update your training with recurring comments. Always ask *'open'* questions, which require a detailed answer rather than asking questions that can be answered with a simple *'yes'* or *'no'*. Writing a training course is an opportunity for you to learn something too.

45. Writing for the UK & US

Webster's dictionary (created in 1828) introduced new American spellings to deliberately separate their cultural identity from that of the British. Make sure you know what language you're writing in.

Words with Double 'l' (UK) or Single 'l' (US)

UK	US
cancelled	canceled
fuelled	fueled
labelled	labeled
signalling	signaling

Words Ending in '-se' (UK) or '-ze' (US)

UK	US
analyse	analyze
organise	organize
recognise	recognize
visualise	visualize

Words Ending in '-ce' (UK) or '-se' (US)

UK	US
defence	defense
licence (noun), license (verb)	license (noun and verb)
offence	offense
Practice (noun), practise (verb)	Practice (noun and verb)

Words Ending in '-re' (UK) or '-er' (US)

UK	US
centre	center
fibre	fiber
metre	meter
theatre	theater

Words Ending in '-our' (UK) or '-or' (US)

UK	US
colour	color
flavour	flavor
labour	labor
rumour	rumor

Different Words & Terms

Some UK words and terms are not used in the US.

UK	US
aerial	antenna
anywhere	anyplace
autumn	fall
dustbin	trashcan
dynamo	generator
engine	motor
holiday	vacation
lift	elevator
mains power	ac power

Units & Abbreviations

In the UK (and Europe), we use the metric (SI Unit) system (metres, kilograms, etc.). The US uses imperial standards (yards, pounds, etc.). If you're writing for the UK, use metric first followed by imperial (in brackets). If you're writing for the US, use imperial first and metric values second (in brackets).

Get an Oxford Dictionary

The Oxford English Dictionary is widely held to be the authority on the English language and includes both UK and US spellings. There are plenty more differences between the two languages in spelling, punctuation and grammar. Don't forget to set the right language on your spellchecker too. Get all the help you can.

DOCUMENT IMAGES

46. Including Meaningful Images

Have a Good Reason for Every Image

Don't add images merely to decorate your document. Always know why you have included an image and make sure it adds value, meaning or information. The exception to this is if you're designing a marketing brochure, or website, and you're using aspirational or emotional images for your readers to identify with.

A diagram is often a better way to present information, show a pattern or explain a relationship, rather than trying to capture it in words. It's always worth taking a little time to see if something is better presented as a diagram.

Include Modified CAD & Engineering Drawings

CAD (Computer-Aided Design) drawings or engineering projections are often inserted in documentation because they are available, but they must earn their place and complement your content. If they contain unwanted detail, unnecessary callouts or spurious information not described in your text, they will likely confuse your readers. Such drawings must always be edited, retouched or redrawn completely to remove extraneous information; otherwise, use them as source information only.

Create Professional-Looking Illustrations

Learning how to use illustration software, or the drawing tools of a word processing application, is time well spent. Amateurish diagrams spoil a document, giving an impression of a lack of professionalism. With illustrations, however, it's not always possible to assign styles to control size, position, alignment, etc., so you'll need to do this manually.

Always make the effort to arrange elements neatly, align boxes and callouts, use consistent line thicknesses, choose same-sized text, etc. Draw images that look smart and consistent, rather than cutting-and-pasting graphics from other sources. Creating slap-dash diagrams indicates laziness and a lack of thought. Setting some formatting rules will ensure your illustrations are consistent and exhibit a professional approach.

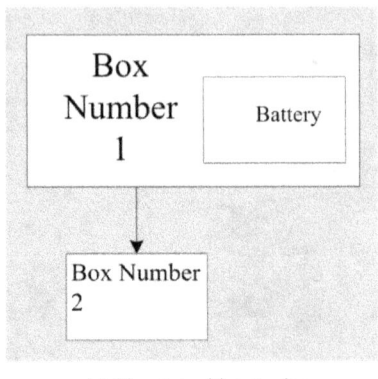
(a) Diagram without rules
(inconsistent)

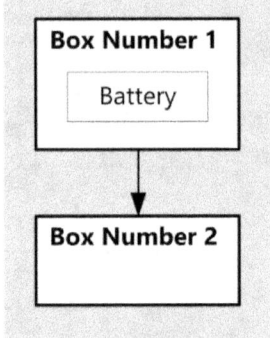
(b) Diagram with rules
(consistent)

Retouch Digital Images

If using a screenshots, photos or other graphics, clean and crop them before for inserting in your document. Learning how to retouch digital images starts with understanding the basics of file types and the difference between raster images and bit maps. Find out which file types best suit your document and specify exactly what you need, when requesting information.

47. Understanding Images

Choosing the right image type and size is important. Too large a file size could slow down the delivery of your online document and too small a file size might look fuzzy when printed.

Raster Images (Illustrations & Drawings)

Raster images are created by software such as Adobe Illustrator® (**.ai**), drawing programs such as Microsoft Visio® (**.vsd**) or computer-aided design applications such as AutoCAD® (**.dwg**).

Generally, you won't insert the **original raster file** in your document since this is a very large file in a special format that assigns properties for every object in the illustration, such as line position, thickness, colour, bend radius, start and end-points, etc. Editing the original file is unlimited using the relevant software application, allowing you to move, reshape and modify objects.

A suitable **output file**, of smaller size, should be generated for inclusion in your document. This will normally be a bitmap file, as described below. Ensure you create a bitmap of suitable resolution for your intended document (screen or print).

If you use the drawing tools within the word processing application, this normally creates a raster image and stores it within the document. You can edit it by clicking on it to reveal the original lines, boxes and text objects.

Bitmaps (Photos & Screen Captures)

Bitmaps are simply images made from small dots (pixels) created by digital cameras and computer screens. When the image is taken, objects in the image cannot be repositioned. Retouching and editing is possible using software such as Adobe Photoshop®:

- **.jpg or .jpeg** (Joint Photographic Experts Group). The quality of the image is degraded when compressed to achieve a smaller file size. Used as a format for photography, it does not support transparency.
- **.gif** (Graphics Interchange Format). Commonly used on social media for static or animated images. The colour range is limited, which keeps the file size small.
- **.bmp** (Bitmap). A Microsoft file format that restricts the colours it stores. A large file size compared to other formats.
- **.png** (Portable Network Graphics). A bitmapped image that doesn't degrade quality when you retouch or re-save it (lossless compression). It supports transparency. File size is generally small, making it ideal for screen or print use.
- **.svg** (Scalable Vector Graphics). Images you can scale to different sizes without compromising the quality. Graphics are good for screen and print use.
- **.tif or tiff** (Tagged Image File Format). Supports RGB and CMYK, which makes them suitable for printing. File size is generally larger than the types listed above.

Always save a copy of your image before editing or retouching. If your editing goes wrong, loses quality, or if you just change your mind, you can always go back to the original.

For images to be used on-screen, you'll need a **low resolution (75-100 dpi)** output file, which will be of relatively small size. For printing, you'll require a **high resolution (300-600 dpi)** file, which will be much larger.

48. Retouching Your Images

When including screenshots, digital photos or web graphics in your document, it's unlikely that they'll be in a good-enough condition for you to insert them as they are. Learning how to edit and retouch bit-map images, will improve the appearance of your documents. Here are ten techniques to consider when retouching any bit map image:

Crop & Re-Frame

Cropping an image will enable you to improve the composition by removing irrelevant detail or space around the edges. The focus of attention can also be altered by re-framing, bringing an object or person closer to the front or more central.

Replace the Background

Changing the environment, or context, of an image by substituting a different background can help make the subject stand out or recede. Applying the same background colour (often white or black is best) can help make all your images consistent.

Rotate the Image

Rotating an image can make a boring image more dynamic by changing vertical and horizontal lines into diagonals, which we perceive as more energetic, drawing the eye in. Alternatively, if a photo you're given has a sloping horizon you'll need to know how to rotate the image to level it.

Adjust Tonal Balance

Dull images can be improved by adjusting the tonal balance so that dark colours are indeed dark and your white tones are truly white. This adjusts the contrast and brightness of your image giving it depth and increasing the dynamic range.

Adjust Colour Balance

Sometimes images can be a little too blue or red, or some other colour. Correcting for a colour cast in your original image will make it appear more realistic and true to life.

Remove Red-Eye, Scratches, Spots & Blemishes

A red-eye tool, cloning tool, smudge tool or paint tool can be used to clean up unwanted marks on your images. Such marks divert attention away from the main subject.

Remove Unwanted Objects

Unwanted objects in an image can sometimes be removed by using the cloning tool, which overlays pixels copied from an alternate area. Take care to select an appropriate region with matching tones, colours or objects that can be safely repeated.

Blur, Blend, Sharpen

When you want the focus to be on a particular subject in an image, you could try to simulate a depth-of-field (a technique used in photography). This blurs unwanted or background objects, making the subject clearer and bringing it into the foreground.

Prepare Print-Ready Images

If you're intending to use the image in a printed document, save as a high-resolution images (300 dpi, or more) to ensure it won't appear fuzzy or jagged when printed.

Prepare Web-Ready Images

If using the image in a website, the resolution can be lower (72-90 dpi) than the printed version. This ensures the file size is kept to a minimum for ease of downloading. Remember to save the original in case you need to amend it in the future.

REVIEWING & EDITING

49. Editing Your First Draft

Before you give your first draft to anyone else to review, do your own editing to ensure there's nothing embarrassing to find. The checks you do will depend on the type of document you're writing. Choose wisely.

Information Checks

Check your information is correct:

- **Completeness** – Make sure you've included all the information you could and haven't missed something that's easy to find out.
- **Accuracy** – Check your facts (and references, if necessary).
- **Headings** – If you have no information on a topic but think there should be something written, include a heading with space in the appropriate place so reviewers can make comments or add information themselves.

Text Checks

Check your writing by re-reading (more than once):

- **Spelling** – Check for words that are spelled correctly but used wrongly, and therefore not picked up by the spellchecker (from/form, etc.).
- **Flow** – Check that you like the way it flows (logical, introducing topics in the correct order and at a pace that your readers can absorb).
- **Tense** – Check that the present tense is used consistently, and appropriately throughout, unless another tense is expressly required.
- **Sentences length** – Check for long and laborious sentences. Mix your sentence length to add variety and interest.
- **Cross-references** – Check that cross-references and hyperlinks are accurate and linking correctly.

Table Checks

Check that all your tables are consistent with correct styles and formatting rules applied:

- **Consistency** – Check rule thickness, text alignment, text size, table numbering, etc.
- **Size/Position** – Check that any long tables breaking across pages occur as intended (consistent use of '*continued*').

Image Checks

Check that all your images are consistent with correct styles and formatting rules applied:

- **Size** – Check your images are sized appropriately.
- **Cropping** – Check whether images could be cropped closer, thus removing excess white space.
- **Quality** – Check image resolution is appropriate for the intended medium (print/screen).
- **Position** – Check whether images would perhaps be better placed on a previous page by reducing their size, if there's a large area of white space.

Design & Format Checks

Check the layout of each page:

- **Consistency** – Check that full-stops, spaces, capitals and punctuation are used consistently, particularly on headings and bulleted lists.
- **Pagination** – Check that no strange page breaks occur. Even if you have set the appropriate widow, orphans and keep-with-next settings, there will probably be some unnatural-looking consequences.
- **Page Numbering** – Check your automatic page numbering has worked correctly.
- **TOC** – Check your table of contents. This should be the last thing to be updated to capture the final pagination.

50. Completing Your First Draft

Highlight Your Comments

Sometimes you won't have all the information you need in your first draft, even after interviewing experts and incorporating source information. Your draft may be incomplete, but don't let this stop you from delivering it.

If there are 'holes' in your content, leave white space and ask for help in filling it from your expert reviewers, such as:

- *"These values require checking, please confirm or let me know where I can get this."*
- *"We need to say something about this. All contributions gratefully received."*
- *"Why is this so? I don't fully understand. More explanation required."*
- *"What does this acronym/term mean? Is it something we use internally or do our customers use it?"*
- *"Image needed here. Where can I get a front panel view?"*

Highlight your questions or requests for information by writing/typing in another colour. **RED + BOLD** always gets people's attention. Your comments will jump off the page and not be mistaken for content. Consider assigning a style for comments to ensure they're always formatted the same way.

Email Your Request for Informtion (RFI)

An alternative to incorporating your own questions and comments in the first draft, is to list them in an email. This can be a quick way to obtain last minute information or to accompany your delivered first draft.

Itemise your comments by page number:

- **Title Page** – Issue date required.
- **Page 1** – Introduction requires front panel view.
- **Page 13** – Specification missing.
- **Page 44** – Explanation/description required.

This provides a useful checklist for you and makes it easier for your reviewer by identifying the affected pages.

Specify a Time Limit

When delivering your draft for review, always specify the date by which you want it returned. This is essential if you are going to stick to your plan and have the document finished by the (already agreed) completion date.

51. Chasing Perfection

First Draft (75% Complete)

A first draft document is roughly 75% of the way to completion. This is as far as you can take it on your first pass, based on the source information you've obtained, the input you've received from technical experts and by accessing the equipment. There may be missing paragraphs or even whole sections. There will be mistakes too, but nothing too embarrassing because you've already checked the document.

Second Draft (95% Complete)

When the first draft is delivered for review by the technical experts, make it clear that this is their one chance to contribute. In addition to correcting and adding technical content, some reviewers will spot spelling mistakes, and that is useful too. When you've incorporated their feedback, insert any last minute updates and re-write paragraphs to hone their effectiveness as you create the second draft. The document is now approximately 95% complete.

Final Draft (99.9% Complete)

The technically reviewed second draft is delivered a higher authority for final review and approval. Again, make it clear that this is management's chance to contribute. Make sure they understand what they are signing off, because they will be responsible in the event of something tragically misrepresented or inaccurate. When you've incorporate their comments in the final draft, the document is 99.9% complete.

There may still be errors present, but they eluded everyone. Be assured, a mistake (or several) will be in there somewhere, which is why I say it's only 99.9% complete. If you have more time, do more checking. You are sure to find something that can be amended or otherwise improved.

Don't Chase the Last 0.1%

It's essential to spend time editing, reviewing and re-writing to catch errors and verify technical accuracy but don't spend an excessive amount of time chasing perfection or delay the delivery. It's always worth delivering the document on time rather than delaying it trying to make it perfect.

Collect & Store Comments

When the document has been issued, that's that. Any mistakes, or additions, which are discovered must be included in the next issue.

Collect customer (reader) feedback, comments and additions by maintaining a marked-up version of the document. Alternatively, store comments in an email or an electronic file, or write a to-do list, so that they can be incorporated in the next issue.

Produce an Amendment or Supplement (if You Really Must)

If there's something critical that must be corrected in your issued document, you could write an Amendment or Supplement and deliver it to all your customers. This will need to reference the document part and issue number and specify the pages affected, so your readers are left in no doubt. Treat this change document as you would any other with drafts and reviews as before.

DOCUMENT MANAGEMENT

52. Keeping Track of Your Document

Is this the Right One?

When creating a document you need to consider how you are going to identify it. Obviously, every document requires a title, but how will you, or anyone else, know that the document they're looking at is the right one, or the latest one, for the product, service or business idea you are delivering. Having just a title is insufficient for describing, storing or publishing it. A little more admin is required.

Just Another Component Part

If the purpose of your document is to support a particular product or service in some way, it can (and should) be considered as just another component part and treated in the same way. It needs to be planned, developed and delivered in the same way, and at the same time; and given the same priority as any other component.

All documents should be treated in the same way if they capture and describe the current state of a design, a product, a service or an idea. It's likely that such documents, even if it's a single drawing, will be stored and retrieved, updated, discussed by colleagues or distributed. In other words, you should make it clear, what it relates to, what aspects it covers, when it was written and by whom.

How to Identify a Document

To identify a document, you need five things:

- **Title** – This should describe the subject and the type of document (e.g. Black Box Installation Guide). Further information, such as a model number, may be included and displayed on the front page.

- **Part Number** – This uniquely identifies the document as a part in the system, which may appear on a BOM (Bill of Materials). If your company has no system for assigning part numbers to documents, assign your own. A straightforward method uses a six-digit code (ABC-001). The three-digit alphabetical code can be used to identify you, your department or the type of document; and the three-digit number enables 999 documents of that type to be created. Placing this code at the start of your file name will help you (and others) to identify documents on your network. Display the part number on the front page, or outside cover, of your document, for easy identification.

- **Issue (Version/Edition) Number** – When a document is first published it will be identified as '*Issue 1*'. If it is updated, it must be up-issued by incrementing the issue number so everyone knows which is the latest version. Place the issue number alongside, or close to, the part number with which it is associated, and at the end of your file name to identify, and store in sequence, the different versions you have produced. If your document is yet to be published, use a draft letter in the same manner, starting at '*A*', to distinguish between versions (drafts) while it is being reviewed.

- **Date** – This indicates when the document was written. Every time the document is up-issued, record the date to let your readers know exactly when it was issued.

- **Author** – This identifies the originator of the document. If readers want to give feedback, add information or correct an error; they will know who to contact and who is responsible for maintaining the document.

53. The Document Lifecycle

After the requirement for a document is conceived, it will need to go through several draft phases while being written, reviewed and approved; before it is published (issued) and becomes an official company document.

A published document is printed, or otherwise delivered or made available, and will continue to exist for as long as it is relevant and accurate. If an important error in the document is noticed that urgently requires fixing, an amendment or supplement can be produced, if absolutely necessary. This must then be delivered to the customers who have the original document. Normally, any changes or updates, while necessary and quite important, can wait for the next issue to be created.

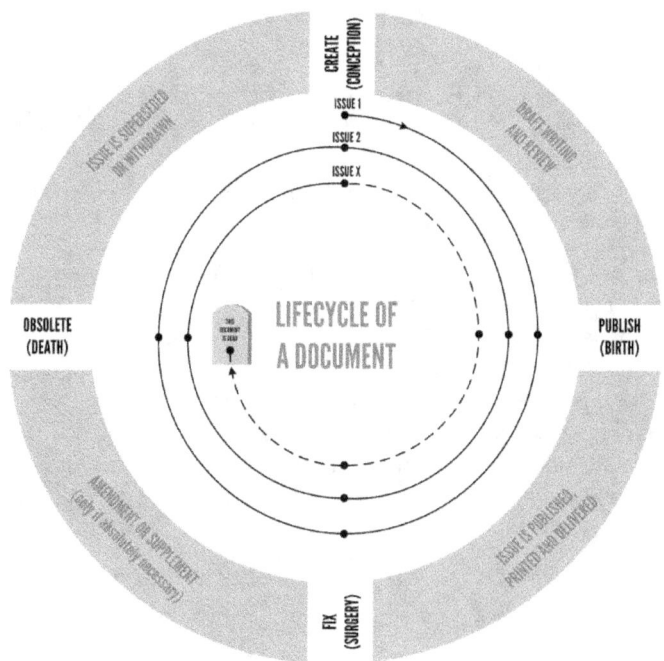

The Document Lifecycle

The issued publication will eventually become obsolete or redundant when significant changes have to be made, perhaps to support new features or ideas. It will remain in circulation, however until a new issue can be written, reviewed, approved and published.

This cycle of up-issuing the document continues until the document itself becomes obsolete and is discontinued. This may reflect the fact that the business idea has been superseded, the product model has been replaced or the service has been withdrawn.

Store Your Masters and Your Reviewed Drafts

It's essential that you store and maintain master files of your documents, along with any illustrations, images, screenshots and cover artworks you have used.

In addition, it's a good idea to keep copies of your draft documents and review comments, so you have a record of the changes made and the information supplied. This will be useful if questions arise about whether comments have been incorporated or not. It also ensures you don't discard any content used in an earlier draft but was removed before publication.

Specialised software is available to control the issue of documents but, if you're able to do basic admin, it's straightforward to manage and control your own documents by labelling folders and files with the appropriate part/draft/issue numbers. Think through what is going to work for you, and allow for future expansion. Having a numbering scheme for identifying your documents allows you to store documents, drafts and issues sequentially (in alphabetical and/or numeric order), rather than just using the name or title.

54. Troubleshooting a Bad Document

If complaints are being received about your documentation, take them seriously; they are useful feedback and can help you create better documents and be a better writer.

Document is Not Being Read

If people are not reading your document, analyse your writing style (Is it easy to follow?), check your navigation (Is it easy to find info?), examine your images (Are they helpful?) and re-read your content (Is it comprehensible?). Can you do anything else to make your content more engaging?

Document is Not Up-To-Date

Ensure you, and your documents, are being kept in the loop. If your document supports a product or service, upgrades and further development should be accompanied by a review (and perhaps an update) of the documentation.

Document Does Not Address the Needs of Reader

If customer support are receiving lots of calls, you might need to broaden the scope of your document or go into more detail. Collect feedback and include the information your readers need.

Document is Vague, Confusing or Misleading

If readers are finding the document confusing, look carefully at your writing. Get your document reviewed and collect feedback. Would additional diagrams, examples or tutorials be helpful?

Document Does Not Match the Product

Check the part number and issue/version number of the document your customers are reading. Do they have the correct documentation for the product or service they are using?

Document Contains Errors/is Inconsist

If there are errors or inconsistencies, do more (better) checking, reviewing and editing. Always allow sufficient time for these essential steps in your writing plan.

Document is Non-Existent

Documentation is often an afterthought, or not provided at all, when a company culture has the belief that it is all intuitive, simple and straightforward. It never is.

Document is Always Late

You can't wait until hardware/software development is completed before writing the documentation. Start sooner. Documentation should be produced in step with product development.

Document is Too Complex

Documentation benefits from the inclusion of examples and tutorials when a concept, a product or an operation is complex. Ensure your customers are able to understand and use those new (and expensive) features that have been developed.

Document is Too Expensive

Doing anything right costs time and money; documentation is no exception. A balance can be struck, however, between what is necessary and what is desirable. Consider using a dedicated technical writer, which will cost less than an engineer or developer. They will also get the job done faster, better and minimise interruptions to important design and development work.

55. Why Bother with Good Documentation?

There are many benefits to taking the time and effort to write good-quality documentation. If written hastily and without thought, it's easy to overlook issues of quality that your readers will notice. They may conclude, not unreasonably, that the sloppy way in which a document is produced probably reflects the quality of the product they're considering buying.

Always remember, when you write something, your personal, departmental and company reputation is on the line.

Delight Your Customers

By providing comprehensive and effective documentation, you'll make your products easier to understand and ensure your customers use them to their full potential.

Reduce Calls to Customer Support

By providing adequate operational, technical and troubleshooting information, you'll reduce the number of calls to customer support as well as the number of problems your customers will have.

Minimise Product Downtime

By providing effective troubleshooting and repair instructions, your customers will be able to rectify faults and get your products (and their services) back online more quickly.

Encourage Repeat Business

By improving customer confidence in your products and product support (your documentation), you'll improve your company's reputation and encourage brand loyalty.

Generate New Business

By supplying a technical publication to a prospective customer as a benchmark of achievement, you add credibility to your sales and marketing literature.

Protect Your Customers

By providing essential health and safety information in your document, your company will fulfil its obligation to provide adequate protection for the end-user.

Protect Your Products

By providing relevant equipment care, installation, handling, operation, storage, and maintenance information, your product will be properly used and maintained by the customer.

Protect Your Company

By recording the functions, features and specifications of the product, you'll provide product liability and patent protection for your company in the event of a dispute.

Train Your Staff

By providing comprehensible and effective structured product documentation, you'll be able to train staff as well as customers.

Increase Company Productivity

By distributing copies of the product manual internally, or making it available on the company intranet, you'll provide a reference for other staff and reduce interruptions to product developers.

What Have You Done?

By immersing yourself in the undertaking of becoming a professional document writer, you will acquire skills and knowledge of other ancillary professions. This opens up a range of potential job opportunities, including:

- Freelance/Contract Writer
- Technical Author/Writer
- Content (Web/Blog) Writer
- Copywriter
- Business Writer
- Bid/Proposal Writer
- Document Editor/Proofreader
- Information Designer
- Instructional Designer
- Graphic Designer
- Illustrator
- Digital Image Editor
- Digital Photographer
- Project Manager

What, at first, may have seemed like a boring and unrewarding assignment, may actually turn out to be a creative opportunity. And all it needed was two things:

- **ATTITUDE** (*"I am going to make an effort"*), and
- **APPRECIATION** (*"I recognise good writing when I read it"*).

Don't forget to update your CV, or resume, with your newly acquired skills and experience.

About the Author

This document represents the knowledge and experience of **Andrew A Moore** acquired during his 30-year career as a *Freelance Technical Author* and *Professional Writer*. Andrew has produced technical and business documentation for numerous UK and US engineering and technology companies. He lives and works in the UK and trades under the name **AAM Design.**

See his website at **www.aamdesign.co.uk** for further information.

www.ingramcontent.com/pod-product-compliance
Lightning Source LLC
Chambersburg PA
CBHW071033240526
45469CB00006BD/2197